ESCAPE TO REALITY - **GREATEST HITS**, VOL. 2

GRACE
CLASSICS

PAUL ELLIS

KINGSPRESS
Birkenhead, New Zealand

Grace Classics: Escape to Reality Greatest Hits, Volume 2

ISBN: 978-1-927230-24-4
Copyright © 2015 by Paul Ellis

Published by KingsPress, Birkenhead, New Zealand. This title is also available as an ebook. Visit www.KingsPress.org for information.

Unless otherwise indicated all Scripture quotations are taken from the Holy Bible, New International Version®, NIV®. Copyright © 1973, 1978, 1984, 2011 by Biblica, Inc.™ Used by permission of Zondervan. All rights reserved worldwide. www.zondervan.com

Scripture quotations marked "AMP" are taken from the Amplified Bible. Copyright © 1954, 1958, 1962, 1964, 1965, 1987 by The Lockman Foundation. Used by permission.

Scriptures quotations marked "GNB" are taken from the *Good News Bible*. Copyright © 1994 published by the Bible Societies/HarperCollins Publishers Ltd UK, *Good News Bible* © American Bible Society 1966, 1971, 1976, 1992. Used by permission.

Scripture quotations marked "KJV" are taken from the *King James Version* of the Bible (1611).

Scripture quotations marked "MSG" are taken from *The Message*. Copyright © by Eugene H. Peterson 1993, 1994, 1995, 1996, 2000, 2001, 2002. Used by permission of NavPress Publishing Group.

Scripture quotations marked "NKJV" are taken from the New King James Version®. Copyright © 1982 by Thomas Nelson, Inc. Used by permission. All rights reserved.

Scripture quotations marked "YLT" are taken from *Young's Literal Translation* of the Bible (1898).

Please note that KingsPress' publishing style capitalizes certain pronouns in Scripture that refer to the Father, Son, and Holy Spirit, and may differ from some publisher's styles.

Cover layout and design by Brad Wallace of bradwallaceimaging.com.

Any Internet addresses printed in this book are offered as a resource. They are not intended in any way to be or imply an endorsement by KingsPress, nor does KingsPress vouch for the content of these sites for the life of this book.

Version: 1.0 (February 2015)

Dedication: This is for Escape to Reality readers whose kindness and patience over the years have helped me sharpen my message.

From E2R Readers

Wow! I consider myself a lifelong student of God's incredible power and grace. Although there are many preachers of grace, I have found none more articulate and clear about the message than Paul Ellis.
- Michael M., real estate investor, Birmingham, AL

I have been greatly blessed by E2R. The clarity of Paul Ellis's explanations and the fixed focus on Jesus just makes me shout "wow!"
- Evans D-M., businessman, Tema, Ghana

I've been a Christian for 13 years but I didn't truly know God until I was exposed to the gospel of grace. Thank you Paul, for proclaiming this truth so boldly on E2R! It has transformed my life and I'm forever grateful.
- Opeyemi P., medical student, Nashville, TN

E2R has been instrumental in my escape from the bondage of legalism and into the freedom of grace. Now my children are learning from Paul Ellis as well and I couldn't be happier.
- Krista F., homeschooling mom, McKinney, TX

In a world that preaches mixture and law, I am left astounded and speechless by the amazing grace that Paul shows. He beautifully goes against cultural-Christian thinking to display the unconditional love of a Dad who wants us just as we are; a Dad that showers us with grace, blessings, favor and love just because we're his. I know now that I am a child rather than a slave because of leaders like Paul!
- Jessi C., college student, Yakima, WA

Paul Ellis does what every great author does – he makes you think outside your box and challenges you to see Jesus in a new way. His message of amazing grace is not only clear but accurately portrays the message the apostles and Jesus died for.

- Zach M., youth pastor, San Antonio, TX

My 30 years as a Christian had been utterly miserable because I had been taught a false grace. I believe our Father brought me to E2R. Grace taught here will blow your mind; it has mine. If you have faulty foundations then pure grace starts to dig them up and lays right foundations. I spent 15 years away from church. If I was at Paul's church I'd be banging on his door and asking for a service every day.

- Bill G., finance director, Winchester, UK

E2R has changed me from religious to gracious, revealing more of Jesus in my life. Kudos brother Paul!

- Jeremiah M., student, Nairobi, Kenya

I have been reading E2R for the past few years. I always look forward to the next post or book! Paul Ellis has a very special gift in writing. The message of the cross is all about grace and Paul captures this essence. I love that he is willing to refute those who oppose in ignorance, yet with grace and love.

- Maryann P., nurse, Clinton, NC

The name of your website has been just that to me, an escape to reality. I have been a Christian for over 30 years. By God's grace and your website, I have been able to rest in God's amazing grace.

- Robert H., store manager, Greensboro, NC

Contents

A word before   1

1. By which gospel are you saved?   5
2. Two religions: Works and blood   10
3. Are you religious?   16
4. Practical holiness — your fast track for setting aside grace   23
5. Whose medicine are you taking? The dangers of taking scripture out of context   30
6. Does God give and take away?   36
7. When doing good is bad for you   43
8. How to walk after the flesh in twenty easy lessons   50
9. Seven signs you might be living under law   58
10. Why repentance is like football   64
11. Why confession is still good for you   70
12. Where was God in the Connecticut school shooting?   76
13. Shipwrecked faith   85
14. What happens to Christians who commit suicide?   92

Bonus track...
15. Star Trek and the Great Commission: Twelve parallels   99

A Word Before

When I was about fourteen years old I was involved in a number of school bands. I wasn't a very good musician, but what I lacked in talent I made up for in volume.

One time the head of the music department asked me and a couple of friends to perform at a Christmas party at a home for intellectually-handicapped people. I was reluctant to go. "We only know two songs." I wasn't joking. Of course, the other band members and I each knew more than two songs, but there were only two songs we knew how to play together. One was Herbie Hancock's classic "Watermelon Man" and the other was the theme to *The Pink Panther*. It wasn't much of a repertoire, but we were just kids.

"Well, just play those two songs," said the head. "You'll be fine." So we went to the home for intellectually-handicapped people and played "Watermelon Man" followed by "The Pink Panther" and then "Watermelon Man" again followed by "The Pink Panther" again and we did this for two straight hours. We tried to mix it up by throwing in extended solos and dramatic finishes, but there was no hiding our limited repertoire.

To our surprise and delight, the audience loved us. Every time we began a new song we heard murmurs of excitement ripple through the crowd. "I know this one!" Maybe they were being kind or perhaps they had genuinely forgotten that we had just played the same song five minutes earlier, but we made a great impression. We were the band that plays the songs everybody knows.

It's possible that the people in that home had not heard "Watermelon Man" or the theme to *The Pink Panther* before that night, but I guarantee those two songs were not quickly forgotten. I like to think they became Christmas classics which are replayed every year.

This experience reminds me of something the apostle Paul said:

> Further, my brothers and sisters, rejoice in the Lord! It is no trouble for me to write the same things to you again, and it is a safeguard for you... Rejoice in the Lord always. I will say it again: Rejoice! (Philippians 3:1, 4:4)

When it came to singing the praises of a good God, Paul was not afraid of playing the same songs again and again. He may have been the smartest guy in the Roman Empire but wherever he went he preached the same simple message, namely, the gospel of God's grace (Acts 20:24). And it is this message that I write about on my blog Escape to Reality (a.k.a. E2R).

A few months ago I released Volume 1 of E2R's Greatest Hits. Welcome to Volume 2. It's great to have you here. The first book was called *Grace Disco*. You may be wondering why this one is called *Grace Classics*.

A classic is something that has stood the test of time and has been judged to be of the highest quality. If this book comes within a million miles of that standard it is because it proclaims the eternal gospel which is the best news and the most thrilling of announcements.

A classic is something that resonates within and fills us with divine beauty. Think of a classic piece of music – Beethoven's *Ode to Joy* comes to mind, so does the hymn *Amazing Grace* – and how it makes you feel when you listen to it. The gospel of grace has the same effect. When we hear it in all its unblemished glory, something within us stirs to life and we lift our eyes to heaven. Our hearts fill with joy and our minds bend with wonder. *Who is this God who loves me like this?*

How can I say that the chapters in this book are – dare I say it – classics? Because each conveys the good news of Jesus and it is *this* message – not my rough versions of it – that has stood the test of time and continues to move those who hear it. I write so that you may rejoice in the Lord who is the embodiment of the Father's love and grace toward us.

The best, most classic bits in this book are not original – I stole them from the Bible. And all the other bits I lifted straight from the blog. But even though you may have read them before, it is no trouble for me to write the same things to you again. Like Paul, I have just one message to preach.

Some of the material on E2R has gone on to shape chapters in my various gospel books. However, most of the articles in this collection of greatest hits have not been published anywhere else. I have taken this opportunity to give them a bit of spit and polish. After each you will find some reflections and stories about how they came to be and how they were received.

If the articles on the blog are the rehearsal, this book is the concert performance. So as the lights go down and the curtain goes up why don't you sit back, relax, and allow the music of God's grace to soothe your soul.

1. By Which Gospel Are You Saved?

Read the New Testament and you might come away thinking that there is more than one gospel. The first words of the New Testament in the King James Bible are, "The Gospel According to Matthew." Read on and you will also find the gospels according to Mark, Luke and John. Keep reading and you will come across Paul telling the Romans about "my gospel" before warning the Corinthians to hold firm to the gospel that "I preached to you" (Romans 16:25, 1 Corinthians 15:1). Read all the way to the end and you will also encounter the "gospel of your salvation" (Ephesians 1:13), the "gospel of peace" (Ephesians 6:15), the "glorious gospel of the blessed God" (1 Timothy 1:11), before finally reaching the "eternal gospel" proclaimed by the angel (Revelation 14:6).

Of course, these are all labels for one and the same gospel. There is only one gospel in the Bible and that is the gospel which was known to Paul as the gospel of grace:

> I consider my life worth nothing to me, if only I may finish the race and complete the task the Lord Jesus has given me — the task of testifying to the gospel of God's grace. (Acts 20:24)

The gospel of grace is *the* gospel and there is no other. This gospel is not built on a doctrine or a theology, but on Jesus Christ himself:

The Word became flesh and made his dwelling among us. We have seen his glory, the glory of the one and only Son, who came from the Father, full of grace and truth… Out of his fullness we have all received grace in place of grace already given. For the law was given through Moses; grace and truth came through Jesus Christ. (John 1:14, 16–17)

Whenever you read the word grace in the Bible, you can substitute the name Jesus for Jesus is grace personified. He is the embodiment of the Father's grace. What does the grace of God look like? It looks like Jesus. What does the grace of God sound like? It sounds like Jesus. How do we know that God is gracious? Because he gave us Jesus who is full of grace and truth.

When Paul refers to the gospel of grace in Acts 20, he means the same thing as when he and others refer to the gospel of *Christ* or the gospel of *God* or the gospel of his *Son* or the gospel of *peace*. All these gospels reveal the One who is called Grace, who was given to us out of the fullness of the Father's grace, and through whom we have received grace upon grace.

What about when Jesus refers to the gospel of the *kingdom* (Matthew 24:14)? Is this a different gospel?

Whenever you hear Jesus talking about the kingdom you can substitute the word "king" because the kingdom is nothing without the king. Who is the king? His name is Jesus. When Jesus says we are to "seek first his kingdom and his righteousness," he is essentially saying "seek me and my righteousness." And where do we find his righteousness? In the gospel of grace:

> For in the gospel the righteousness of God is revealed—a righteousness that is by faith from first to last, just as it is written: "The righteous will live by faith." (Romans 1:17)

To sum up, the gospel of the kingdom is the gospel of Christ which is the gospel of God which is the gospel of grace. They are different labels for the exact same gospel message.

So what is the gospel of grace? Paul summarized the gospel of grace like this:

> Now, brothers and sisters, I want to remind you of the gospel I preached to you, which you received and on which you have taken your stand. *By this gospel you are saved...* For what I received I passed on to you as of first importance: that Christ died for our sins according to the Scriptures, that he was buried, that he was raised on the third day according to the Scriptures...
> (1 Corinthians 15:1–4, emphasis added)

What are the three most important bits of the gospel message according to its most prolific preacher? They are; (i) that Christ died for our sins as foretold in the Scriptures, (ii) he was buried, and (iii) he was raised as the prophets foretold.

On the cross Jesus bore our sin and secured our eternal forgiveness. He died so that we might live, was wounded that we might be healed, and he was cursed that we might be blessed.

Jesus forged a new covenant in his blood, exchanging our sinfulness for his righteousness. His miraculous return from death confirmed that Jesus is God's Son, just as he said he was. It also showed that the demands of justice had been fully satisfied and that no further payment was necessary.

The gospel is good news whether you believe it or not, but it will only benefit you if you believe it. Paul said to the Corinthians, "by this gospel are you saved." By which gospel? By the gospel of God's grace:

> For it is by grace you have been saved, through faith — and this not from yourselves, it is the gift of God — not by works, so that no one can boast. (Ephesians 2:8–9)

The gospel is no mere message. It is heaven's cure for the world's woes. And we can be fully confident that God's cures are effective! Those who trust in his goodness and grace experience salvation power in all its fullness — victory over sin, healing from sickness, and freedom from oppression.

> For I am not ashamed of the gospel, because it is the power of God for the salvation of everyone who believes... (Romans 1:16a)

The gospel is not just good news for the sinner. It is good news for the sick, the prisoner and the poor. It's even good news for Christians.

A word after

I didn't know this until I wrote the above article, but it turns out that some people believe there are *two* gospels — one for Israel and another for the Gentiles. Apparently the Jewish apostles (Peter, James, John, etc.) preached the former, while Paul preached the latter. I'm not so sure about this. Paul said that anyone who preached another gospel was accursed (Galatians 1:8). If the apostles had different gospels, then the New Testament writers are a house divided.

What we can say is that there are different audiences and different ways of presenting the eternal gospel of grace. There are many people but only one body, one Spirit, one Lord, one faith, one baptism, one God and Father of all (Ephesians 4:4–6). The angel brought good news of great joy for *all* people and that good news is *the* one and only gospel of Jesus Christ.

9

2. Two Religions: Works and Blood

Travel the world and you could be forgiven for thinking there are thousands of religions and belief-systems. But in reality there are only two: religion based on your works and religion based on the blood of Jesus. People waste years studying different religions trying to figure out which one is best. But strip away all the packaging and you're left with a simple choice: it's your works or his blood.

From the time of Cain men have been trying to impress God with the fruits of their labor. And from the time of Cain God has been rejecting their offerings:

> The Lord looked with favor on Abel and his offering, but on Cain and his offering he did not look with favor. (Genesis 4:4b–5a)

Abel offered the firstborn of his flock while Cain brought a fruit basket. Why was Abel's offering accepted while Cain's was not?

> By faith Abel offered to God a more excellent sacrifice than Cain, through which he obtained witness that he was righteous… (Hebrews 11:4 NKJV)

Abel's sacrifice revealed his faith. Since faith is always a response to something God has said or done, we could ask, what was Abel responding to? He was responding to the sacrificial gift God had given to Adam and Eve in the Garden.

While Abel's faith was a response to what God had done, Cain's faith was in the work of his own hands. Abel considered what God had done, but Cain wanted God to look at what *he* had done. Big mistake. Instead of responding to God in faith, Cain tried to forge his own religion and was rejected.

Two brothers, two religions

Religion based on human effort is unacceptable to God. You can toil and serve and bring costly sacrifices every day of your life but it will not improve your standing before him one bit. You cannot buy your salvation with acts of charity. You cannot bribe your way into his good books with acts of righteousness.

Of course this does not mean you should go out and slaughter some poor sheep. The blood of animals does nothing to take away our sins (Hebrews 10:4). Before the cross these things only had value because they pointed ahead to the blood of Jesus. We live after the cross. The Lamb of God has come and his one-time sacrifice was more than enough to account for all the sins of the world (Hebrews 9:26).

Just as there are only two religions, there are two kinds of preacher; those who say we are qualified by works and those who say we are qualified by the blood of Jesus. These two preachers may look the same, but their messages could not be more different. Consider the following contrasts…

The Works-Preacher says you have to do stuff to stay saved. Make a mistake and you're lost for eternity.

The Blood-Preacher says Jesus' blood has obtained your eternal and complete redemption (Hebrews 9:12). Nothing can separate you from the love of God.

WP: Don't touch! Don't handle! Touch no unclean thing and be holy.

BP: You are sanctified by the blood of the covenant (Hebrews 10:29). We separate ourselves from unclean things not to become holy but because we are holy and what fellowship does light have with darkness?

WP: You have to overcome in life's trials and dress yourself in white clothes, otherwise Jesus will blot out your name.

BP: It's not about you. Jesus is your victory! Wash your filthy self-righteous clothes in the cleansing blood of the Lamb (Revelation 7:14). Rejoice, because he promised to never blot out your name.

WP: Say your prayers and have a regular quiet time because if you don't remain in him, he'll lop you off and throw you into the fire.

BP: Jesus said, "Whoever drinks my blood remains in me, and I in him" (John 6:56). Remaining in Christ is not about what you do but what you believe (see 1 John 4:15). Those who come to him he will never cast away (John 6:37).

WP: Beware of sin! It desires to be your master, so avoid it and run from those who have it.

BP: Be Christ-conscious, not sin-conscious. His sacrifice did away with sin and you have been set free from its power by his blood (Hebrew 9:26, Revelation 1:5). Live free from fear and condemnation.

WP: When you sin, you need to confess to get forgiven again.

BP: You were forgiven 2000 years ago (Colossians 2:13). Your forgiveness is not based on your confession but his blood (Matthew 26:28). True confession is agreeing with God about who he is and what he has done.

WP: When you sin, you need to confess to get clean and clear your guilty conscience. Ask the Holy Spirit to examine you and point out your shortcomings.

BP: The blood of Jesus cleanses and keeps on cleansing you (1 John 1:7). It is the only effective guilt remover (Hebrews 10:19–22). The Holy Spirit will seek to convince you of your righteousness in Christ (John 16:10).

WP: God is holy and lives in unapproachable light. Don't even think about drawing near.
BP: You who were once far away have been brought near through the blood of Christ (Ephesians 2:13).

Are you listening to Pastor Cain or Pastor Abel? Is your faith in the death-dealing works of religion or in the life-giving blood of Jesus Christ? Are you striving to earn God's favor or are you resting in the finished work of the cross?

It makes no difference whether you're Catholic or Protestant, Episcopalian, Baptist or a member of the Western Branch of American Reform Presbyluther-anism. If you are standing on the blood of Jesus, then you are completely forgiven, you are acceptable, and God's favor rests on you!

A word after

This was one of the first articles I posted on E2R and the reaction it elicited taught me the amazing, stun-ning, and super power of making contrasts. Readers loved these distinctions and I can understand why. To grasp grace it's often helpful to see what grace isn't. Indeed, the Bible does this for it tells us that grace isn't works, grace isn't law, grace isn't a lot of things.

Yet contrasts such as these are not often heard in a religious culture that esteems balance and moderation. Instead, we hear things like, "It's grace plus works," or "God gives us grace to keep his commands," or "If you confess, he will be gracious to forgive you." These mixed-up messages lead to mixed-up thinking. "Sometimes God loves me, sometimes he's angry with me. Sometimes he blesses me, sometimes he curses me."

As much as I love the gospel of grace, I hate the message of mixture. I hate how it distorts the white-hot love of our Father and paralyzes those who receive it. And this is why I'm thankful for all the contrasts in scripture. I'm glad we have Cain and Abel, Esau and Jacob, Hagar and Sarah, Mt Sinai and Mt Zion, first Adam and last Adam. In a world of mixture dividing lines help us to separate the pure gospel of heaven from the earthly additives that ruin it.

3. Are You Religious?

Religion can be defined as man's attempt to impress God through self-improvement. It is an attitude that says, "I can make something of myself, I can earn God's favor." This mindset is fatally opposed to the grace of God. It causes a man to stand when he should bow and to strut when he should kneel. Worst of all, it causes him to see himself as a co-savior. His motives may be sincere, but he is an idol-worshipper.

Jesus didn't suffer and die on the cross to make you religious. He died and rose again to give you a new life—*his* life. Anything that pretends to be a substitute for the thrill of knowing him—of trusting him, being with him, and walking with him—should be rejected as inferior.

Are you religious? On the next page is a simple test to find out. If any of the statements in the test describes you, then you might be a little bit religious. Here's why…

Are you preoccupied with doing the right thing?

God is looking for relationship, but a religious mind-set is preoccupied with following the rules. "Just tell me what to do and I will do it." Whether you define the "right thing" as the 10 commandments, the words of Jesus, your church traditions, or whatever, living by a code of conduct is infinitely inferior to the life Christ wants to live through us. It is eating from the wrong tree.

Are You Religious?

T F

☐ ☐ I always try to do the right thing

☐ ☐ I act as if God is keeping score

☐ ☐ I often think about my sins

☐ ☐ I am motivated by a sense of duty

☐ ☐ I live in holy fear of God's anger

☐ ☐ I like doing things for God

☐ ☐ I see myself primarily as a servant of God

An independent spirit, such as Adam had, wants to decide for himself and thus prefers rules to relationship. But someone under grace says, "I trust him from start to finish. He will lead me in the way of life."

Your choice is rules or relationship. You cannot reduce relationship to a set of rules. (Try it with your marriage and see how far that gets you!) Live by the rules and you're setting yourself up for failure, for any kind of law will stimulate sin and lead to your defeat (Romans 7:9). Even when you do the right thing it'll be the wrong thing because you'll be walking in the flesh instead of walking by faith. But when you choose to abide in Christ you'll find yourself doing the right thing at the right time every time.

Do you act as if God is keeping score?

A performance mentality is central to every manmade religion: Do good, get good. Do bad, get bad. The problem with this is your best is not good enough. If God was keeping score, all of us would fall short. The religious mindset invariably leads to performance anxiety. God expects perfection and nothing less. So either you must deliver a perfect performance or you must put your faith in a perfect high priest.

Are you sin-conscious?

Sin-consciousness is the strongest indicator of a religious mindset. Through his one-time sacrifice Jesus has done away with all sin (1 John 2:2, Hebrews 9:26). Sin was a problem, but because of Jesus it is no longer a problem. So what is the problem? The problem is whether you will choose to believe in the all-sufficiency of Christ and his work or trust in yourself and yours. Religion will keep the focus on you and your unworthiness, but grace focuses on Christ and his worthiness.

Are you motivated by your Christian duty?

Religion cries, "Jesus died for you. What will you do for him?" I would do anything for Jesus, but if my motivation is a perceived debt, then I've missed grace.

Whether it's disguised as duty or responsibility, a religious person fundamentally believes that he is obligated or indebted to God. Such a person wants to work so that they no longer owe him. Indeed, they want God to owe them. They want to be in a position where God will have to bless them because of what they've done. This debt-consciousness is opposed to the grace of God for grace comes with no strings attached. There is no *quid pro quo* in a love-based relationship. The believer who has been apprehended by love does not serve out of duty but delight.

Do you fear God's anger?

Listen to the mixed-up messages of manmade religion and you may get the impression that God is a temperamental and abusive Father who sometimes lashes out in fits of righteous wrath. In this scenario Jesus is a sort of go-between who stands in the gap and takes our blows. But the truth is that God the Father, Son and Spirit are perfectly united in purpose and character. If you want to know what God the Father is like, look at the Son (Hebrews 1:3).

How could God get angry with us when he has promised not to be angry ever again (Isaiah 54:9–10)? At great personal cost God the Father and God the Son forged an eternal and unshakeable covenant of peace. We are the beneficiaries of this covenant. Why did he do it? Because he is your Father and he loves you. When you have seen his love, any fear of punishment will evaporate (1 John 4:18).

Do you like doing things for God?

Contrary to what religion has told you, we are not called to work *for* God but to do the work *of* God (John 6:29). Big difference. Working for God reveals our initiative, but faith is always a response to what God is doing or has done.

The Bible distinguishes dead works from good works. Dead works are those that seem right to us but which lead to death. Good works are those which have been prepared by God in advance for us to do (Ephesians 2:10). Dead works require no faith — if you have the resources you can do them. Good works always reveal the Father and may involve healing the sick, raising the dead, cleansing lepers, and driving out demons (Matthew 10:8). As always, Jesus is our role model. He did nothing on his own but lived a full and fruitful life in response to the Father (John 5:19).

Do you see yourself mainly as a servant of God?

Here is the question that separates the religious from the righteous: Do you see God as your heavenly Father, your *Papa*? The religious will hesitate to speak of the Almighty in such familiar terms. They prefer say, "I would rather be a doorkeeper in the house of my God" and so forth. Thinking it sufficient to be a servant, the religious miss out on the best thing of all.

There are only two kinds of people in the world: sons and orphans. Which are you? Religion will leave you so confused about your identity that you will relate to God in any way except as a son, yet Jesus came to reveal God your Father.

Like the prodigal, you may see yourself as nothing more than a servant. Perhaps you left the pig trough with a prepared speech that began, "make me like one of your hired hands" (Luke 15:19). But God is not interested in that speech! Nor is he recruiting servants. God sees you as a son (Galatians 4:6). Don't argue with your Father.

A word after

When someone says "I'm a servant of God," what they may mean is "I serve God." Did you ever stop to ponder the audacity of that statement? God created the universe with nothing but *words*. What need does he have for servants? In what capacity *could* we possibly serve him? If the God who sustains all things by his word went on holiday, we couldn't keep the universe running for a millisecond. "What happened? I was only gone for a minute."

When Paul identifies himself as a servant of Christ, as he does at the start of some of his letters, he is saying that he serves in the manner in which Christ served. He's saying, "I serve people in the Name of

Jesus." True, Paul does talk about serving God on occasion, but how exactly did it he do that? What form did his service take?

> God, whom I serve with my whole heart in preaching the gospel of his Son... (Romans 1:9)

Paul considered preaching the gospel as service to God. That's a neat way to define service because God doesn't actually need to hear the good news. He invented it! But when we preach the gospel of his Son, God is blessed because his family increases. He gets more sons and daughters. So one of the best ways we can serve God and others is by proclaiming the good news of Jesus.

4. "Practical Holiness"—
Your Fast-Track for Setting Aside Grace

Life under the old covenant was so much simpler than the free and confusing world of grace. Back then if you wanted to stay on the straight and narrow, you just had to keep all the rules. But in the kingdom of grace, there are no rules (1 Corinthians 6:12). A good marriage doesn't need them. For those unacquainted with the security of God's love, the absence of rules can be terrifying. "Help! Somebody tell me what to do! I need rules!"

Enter the holiness preachers.

Much of what passes for holiness preaching today is old covenant theology dressed up in new covenant ribbons. See if you can spot the difference:

Then: God promised we would be his holy people if we kept the rules. In other words, *the rules are a manual for holiness.*

Now: Am I saved by the law? Oh, good heavens no. That's so old covenant. I don't keep the law to earn salvation. But the law does show me how to please the Lord. In other words, *the rules are a manual for holiness.*

Do you see the difference? Strip away the mumbo-jumbo and there is no difference! Just read some of the comments I get whenever I talk about the commands of Jesus and you will find 101 different ways of saying the same thing: *The rules are a manual for holy living.*

The only difference between then and now is that some of the rules have changed. The Israelites lived by the ceremonial rules of Moses; today, many Christians make up their own rules. "I obey the red letters of Jesus." "I try to do everything in the Bible." "I just do whatever my pastor says."

D.I.Y. holiness

Practical holiness is a term to beware as it often comes hiding a fishhook. Much of it is pure mixture, as the following soundbites illustrate:

- "Following Christ is a lifestyle." (True.) "We've got to keep his commands to be his disciples." (Nope — that's backwards. That's putting the fruit before the tree.)
- "Find out what pleases the Lord." (Okay!) "Keeping his instructions pleases him." (But that's a recipe for the sort of faithless, law-based living that nullifies grace and inflames sin. Jesus pleases the Lord. Trust him.)
- "If you sow to the flesh you will reap destruction." (Yep). "So we have to be earnest in getting people to improve themselves and modify their behavior." (But that's sowing to the flesh! You're setting them up for failure.)

24

Holiness preaching that emphasizes *what you must do* is carnal Christianity. Make no mistake, it comes straight out of the old covenant. Heed this sort of teaching and you will exalt the flesh at the expense of grace. And it won't make you holy.

There are at least four ways to determine whether the holiness message you're listening to reflects the condemning covenant of the law or the new and liberating covenant of grace:

- Old covenant holiness is based on who you are and is sold as a list of things you must do; new covenant holiness is based on who Christ is (our holiness – 1 Corinthians 1:30) and what he has done (sanctified you – Romans 11:16).
- Old covenant holiness emphasizes imperfect sacrifices you are expected to make; new covenant holiness emphasizes the perfectly perfect sacrifice of the Lamb, by which you have been "perfected forever" (Hebrews 10:14).
- Old covenant holiness is sold as a process of progressive sanctification – something "we grow into" as we become more like Christ; new covenant holiness is presented as a done deal and something to live out (1 Corinthians 1:2).
- Old covenant holiness comes with a big stick – "the Lord may condemn you if you don't deliver"; new covenant holiness has exhortations but no sticks because there is no condemnation to those who are in Christ Jesus (Romans 8:1).

Beware frowners preaching holiness

Because of these differences in message, we can also recognize differences in the messenger. An old covenant holiness preacher will come across as serious and threatening. He will remind you of Moses warning the Israelites at the foot of Mt Sinai. But a new covenant holiness preacher will come across as life-giving and inspirational. He will remind you of Jesus speaking the words of eternal life. An old covenant preacher will speak the faithless language of longing and lack. But a new covenant preacher will bracket any exhortations with affirmations like these:

> As for other matters, brothers and sisters, we instructed you how to live in order to please God, *as in fact you are living...* (1 Thessalonians 4:1a, emphasis added).

> Now about your love for one another we do not need to write to you, for you yourselves have been taught by God to love each other. And *in fact, you do love* all of God's family throughout Macedonia. (1 Thessalonians 4:9–10a, emphasis added)

How to preach holiness

One day I plan to do a series on how to preach holiness the same way the apostles did it. For those who can't wait, here's the short version: To be holy is to partake of his wholeness; it is to stop acting broken (because in him we are not broken) and to allow him to express his whole and beautiful life through us.

The challenge is that being holy is a new experience for us. As sinners, our lifestyle was characterized by brokenness and hurt. Holy living was alien to us. Now that we are in him we have to learn to walk in our new and God-given identity.

The wrong way to approach this is to think of yourself as a flawed sinner trying to become holy. That's not who you are and that's not how it works. Instead, see yourself as a toddler learning to walk. Just as you wouldn't spank an infant if they stumbled and fell, neither will your heavenly Father spank you. He doesn't condemn you when you fall; he encourages you to get up and walk!

He has given you everything you need for life and godliness. In Christ you lack nothing. You just need to work out who you already are and what he has already given you. This is the adventure of holy living.

A word after

A reader asked me whether we should give grace to believers when all is going well, but when they're not doing well give them law so they'll be driven back to grace. This is a bad idea for we are to live under grace, not a mixture of law and grace. Grace is not a reward to be doled out for good behavior or withdrawn for bad. Turn the priceless grace of God into a carrot and it ceases to be grace. Grace is like oxygen. We need it to live, in good times and bad.

Paul said "the law was added so that the trespass might increase" (Romans 5:20a). Give law to a struggling believer and things will go from bad to worse. The law will do to their sin what kerosene does to a flame.

What draws people to grace? Grace does (see John 12:32). Grace is the most attractive force in the universe and anything we add to it only diminishes its drawing power.

The Good Shepherd calls his sheep by name and they come. He does not need "the sheepdog of the law" to round them up.

The law is not your sheepdog, watchdog or guide dog. The law was put in place to lead you to Christ so that you might be justified by faith (Galatians 3:24). Have you come to Christ? Have you been born again? Then you have no further need of the law. It has done its job. Paul says the law was not made for the righteous (1 Timothy 1:9), and in Christ *you are righteous*. In Christ you are also holy (Hebrews 10:10).

"But what happens if I act unholy? Don't I need the law to set me straight?" No, that is not the law's purpose. As DL Moody may have said, "The law tells me how crooked I am. Grace comes along and straightens me out."

You were not made holy by keeping the law and you are not made unholy by breaking it. You are holy because the Holy One lives in you. And if the Vine be holy, then so are his branches.

5. Whose Medicine Are You Taking?
The Dangers of Taking Scripture Out of Context

Two men go to see the doctor. The first is suffering from advanced cancer and needs a life-saving intervention. The second is completely healthy and is going for a routine check-up. The doctor is a perfect physician and prescribes the appropriate medication in each case.

However, the pharmacist bungles the prescriptions and gives each man the other's medicine. The man with cancer is given multivitamins and told to exercise daily, while the healthy man is given an extensive course of chemotherapy. Unsurprisingly, the sick man dies from taking the wrong pills while the healthy man suffers unnecessarily.

In this parable the perfect physician represents Jesus. Jesus knows our every need and always prescribes the perfect medicine.

For the self-righteous person that medicine might be a judicious application of the law. The law is good if used properly and its purpose is to break our pride, silence our self-righteousness, and reveal our need for a Savior. Ultimately the law is meant to lead us to Jesus so that we may receive the gift of his righteousness (Galatians 3:24, Romans 5:17).

But the law is of no use to the saint who has already been set free from the cancer of sin. The ritualistic observance of regulations does nothing to promote godly living and enslaves the free

(Colossians 2:23). The best medicine for saints is a healthy dose of God's grace supplemented with the daily exercise of faith.

In the parable the confused pharmacist represents the preacher (or writer!) who mistakenly gives grace to the self-righteous and law to saints. The result is that both will be made worse off. The self-righteous unbeliever will be led to believe that all is well even as death reaches for him, while the saint will be led to believe that eternity hinges on his ability to deliver a good performance for Jesus. Instead of walking in the freedom that Christ brings, he will come under guilt and condemnation as he strives, and fails, to live at Christ's level. He will be miserable and his hair will fall out from stress.

The Bible is a repository of life-saving medicine, but confused preachers sometimes mix up the medicine. With the best of intentions they do more harm than good.

An example from Peter

Let me give you an example from the three chapters of 2nd Peter. In chapter 1 Peter expounds on the forgiveness, grace and power that come from God. In chapter 2 Peter warns the church about the false prophets and false teachers who are "among you" (v.1). What do these guys look like? Peter says they are those who follow the way of Balaam (v.15), are "slaves of depravity" (v.19), and who know about

Jesus but "never stop sinning" (v.14). In short they are sinners who know about the things of God (like Balaam did), who are acquainted with the "way of righteousness," but they've turned their backs on it (v.21) and so remain under condemnation (v.3). Peter distinguishes these "unrighteous" men from the "godly men that God rescues from trials" (v.9).

In chapter 3 Peter turns his attention back to the saints four times referring to them as his "dear friends." If chapter 2 is full of fury at the ungodly infiltrating positions of leadership within the church, chapter 3 contains fatherly exhortations for the saints.

Problems arise when the medicine-dispensers confuse the dear friends of chapter 3 with the slaves of depravity of chapter 2. Harsh, condemning words meant for the self righteous are spoken over those whom Christ calls righteous. Instead of being warned about the dangers of listening to false teachers and prophets, the saints are treated as if they were false themselves. Like the healthy man in the parable, they are given medicine that is not meant for them and the result is they are left in a worse position than when they came in.

An example from Jude

Like Peter, Jude similarly draws a line between "god-less men" who deny Jesus Christ as Lord and his "dear friends" who are loved and kept by Jesus. It's important to note that both types of people can be found attending church meetings for Jude says of these godless men that they have "slipped in among you" (v.4).

Again, in the hands of a confused preacher, Jude's warning *for* the saints can be twisted into a warning *to* the saints. But Jude's message is "woe to *them*" (v.11), not "woe to you." Jude's medicine of rebuke is specifically for the godless Christ-denier who remains under condemnation, not the saint who is justified by Jesus.

The punch-line of Jude's letter is one of the clearest assurances a Christian can have that they are righteous, sanctified and kept safe by Jesus:

> To him who is able to keep you from stumbling and to present you before his glorious presence without fault and with great joy — to the only God our Savior be glory, majesty, power and authority, through Jesus Christ our Lord, before all ages, now and forevermore! Amen. (Jude 1:24–25)

A word after

"Paul, are you saying we should give the law to sinners? I thought we were supposed to tell them the good news!" I totally agree. We are to proclaim the good news of God's love and grace to the nations. But not everyone will receive it. Those who are smug in their self-righteousness or hardened by sin may not be receptive to the good news of God's grace. In such cases, the law may serve a purpose, as Paul explains in 1 Timothy 1:8–11. The law is good for breaking the hard heart of the proud so that it may become receptive to grace.

We are not in the business of dividing people into camps, yet Peter seems to do exactly this in the second chapter of his letter. So do the other apostles when they distinguish *us* (e.g., dear friends, saints, beloved) from *them* (the unrighteous, slaves of depravity, etc.). Surely God loves the whole world and Jesus died for everyone, but not everyone loves Jesus, hence these distinctions. People divide themselves by their response to grace. Peter is just telling it like it is.

But what does it mean to leave the straight way and wander off as these false prophets did (2 Peter 2:15). In what sense did they "know about the way of righteousness?" Is Peter saying they were once saved but fell from their secure position? Not at all. He is simply saying that they had heard about Jesus (v.20) but rejected him. They remained unrepentant and unchanged by grace.

Note the strong language that Peter uses to describe these false prophets. He says they are still living in the dog-eat-dog world of ungrace (v.22). They are "brute beasts, creatures of instinct, born only to be caught and destroyed" (v.12). Peter is not describing saints but unrighteous men (v.9) who deny Jesus (v.1), follow Balaam (v.15), remain slaves to depravity (v.19) and who never stop sinning (v.14). I don't believe Peter hates these guys, but he surely hates their antichrist message and damaging influence.

Peter's words for them should not scare you. You don't follow Balaam and you have not denied Jesus. Indeed, you are his living, shining testimony of grace.

6. Does God Give and Take Away?

The entire Bible is good for you, but you won't get much out of it unless you know Jesus Christ. To understand the written word, you need to know the Living Word. Try to read the Bible without an appreciation of Jesus—who he is and what he has done—and you may end up taking someone else's medicine. Some verses will appear to contradict others and you will get confused.

Today I want to look at a man who believed that God gives us good gifts only to take them away again. You can probably guess that I'm talking about Job. Job had this one really bad week when his livestock were stolen, his servants were slain, and his kids were killed when a house fell on them. For some reason, Job thought God was behind his loss for he said:

> The Lord gave and the Lord has taken away; may the name of the Lord be praised. (Job 1:21)

If there was ever a scripture that has led to some screwy notions about God's character, it's this one. Anyone who has suffered loss has probably heard this verse. It's often quoted at funerals. We even sing songs about it. For some strange reason people seem to find comfort in believing that God is responsible for their loss.

Now don't get me wrong—I love Job's attitude. He's saying that whatever happens in life, he's going to praise the name of the Lord. But Job still said some dumb things about God. By his own admission he spoke of things he did not understand (see Job 42:3).

But the question stands: Does God give and take away?

Any picture we have of God needs to be informed by Jesus Christ. Jesus is the "radiance of God's glory, the exact representation of his being" (Hebrews 1:3). To get a good understanding of God's character, we need to look to Jesus, not Job. Can you imagine Jesus stealing or killing? Of course not. So how is it that some people think that God was responsible for Job's loss?

"But Paul, it's in the Bible, it's right there in black and white – 'the Lord gave and the Lord has taken away'." Let me put it to you like this. If you want the best insight into God's character, are you better off looking at Jesus, who said "anyone who has seen me has seen the Father" (John 14:9), or Job, who by his own admission, did not really know him (see Job 42:5)? It seems obvious that Jesus is the better choice.

Jesus came to reveal God the great giver (see John 3:16). Have you been given something good? Then see God as your source. He gave it to you:

Every good and perfect gift is from above, coming down from the Father of the heavenly lights, who does not change like shifting shadows. (James 1:17)

But what if you have suffered loss, like Job? He lost his health, his wealth, and his family. The temptation may be to blame God for your loss, as if God had a change of heart. But God is not fickle. He does not change like shifting shadows. He is an extraordinary giver who never takes back his gifts.

> God's gifts and God's call are under full warranty—never canceled, never rescinded. (Romans 11:29, MSG)

So if God is doing the giving, who is doing the taking? Jesus tells us:

> The thief comes only to steal and kill and destroy; I have come that they may have life, and have it to the full. (John 10:10)

We ought not to be confused about these two different roles. One is a giver, the other is a taker. If you have been given something good, then give thanks to God. But if you've been robbed, don't blame God. He is not behind your loss.

Humans can be spectacularly slow learners. From the beginning of history the devil has been trying to steal or ruin everything God has ever given us and yet there are still some who think that God is the thief! God gave us authority over a planet and the devil took it. God gave us freedom and the devil somehow got us to swap that for slavery. God gave us eternal life, health and glory, and we lost it all. But thank God for Jesus who took back what the devil stole!

Jesus came to reveal a generous Father and to destroy the work of the thief (1 John 3:8). Jesus came that we might have life to the full, not to the half.

If you think that God gives and takes away, then you have more faith in karma than grace. Karma says that what goes around comes around. If you're healthy now, you'll be sick tomorrow. If you're prospering now, poverty's waiting around the next corner. Trust in karma and you won't be surprised when disappointments and hardships come. You'll just throw in the towel and say, "I knew it was too good to last."

The world works according to the principle of give and take, but God just gives. The only thing he'll take off you — if you let him — is your sin, your shame, your sickness, your worries and your fears. He takes away those things that harm us and only gives us good things that bless us.

Are you a Job or a David?

Like Job, David was also robbed (see 1 Samuel 30:1–5). And like Job, David was greatly distressed and surrounded by faithless friends with bad advice. But unlike Job, David did a Jesusy-thing and took back what was stolen.

Why did David fight while Job quit? We are told that David "encouraged himself in the Lord his God"

(1 Samuel 30:6). In his pain David considered God's goodness and realized that God was not behind his loss. He understood that it was not God's will for him to suffer, so he fought back and prevailed.

I wish I could go back in time and get to Job before his friends did. I would say, "Job, God didn't kill your kids! He didn't steal your livelihood and make you sick. You've been robbed. Don't sit there in the ashes and cry about it, get up and fight! Are you a warrior or a weakling? Are you a victor or a victim?"

The church will never see victory if we think God is behind our suffering. If we think God is robbing us we won't even resist. We'll let the thief waltz in and plunder our families all the while singing "He gives and takes away."

Funny, but I can't imagine Jesus or David doing that.

For too long we have been incapacitated by uncertainty which is really just another name for unbelief. If you are uncertain who is behind your suffering don't look to Job. Instead look to Jesus who was never confused about who was giving and who was taking.

A word after

Without a doubt, this is the most polarizing article I have ever written. Readers either loved or hated it. Those who hated it typically did so for one of four reasons.

(1) "Paul, how can you say Job spoke out of line? Job was a saint!" Hey, I'm just agreeing with God and Elihu (Job 38:2, 32:12). Even Job came to realize that he had spoken inappropriately (Job 42:3). I'm not condemning Job for what he said in his hour of grief. I'm marveling at the mercy of God who intervened and helped Job to change his tune. I'm in awe of the way God's grace turns our laments into praise.

(2) "Job is an example for us to follow." Not when he's going the wrong way. Job was fearful, superstitious, self-righteous, bitter, and had a death wish. Why would you want to follow him? Follow Jesus!

(3) "Job 1:8 says the whole thing was a set-up. God gave Satan permission." Read that passage in a literal translation and you will find it says no such thing:

> And Jehovah saith unto the Adversary, "Hast thou set thy heart against my servant Job because there is none like him in the land, a man perfect and upright, fearing God, and turning aside from evil?" (Job 1:8, YLT)

Satan came gunning for Job. Why didn't God stop him? We might also ask why God doesn't stop

earthquakes or famines or wars. Not everything
that happens is God's will. Satan went for Job
because he could. When God said, "All that he
has is in thy power" (Job 1:12), he wasn't handing
Job over to Satan—God doesn't do deals with the
devil. He was simply stating a fact (see 1 John
5:19). If Satan had to ask permission, he wouldn't
be a thief would he?

(4) "God is sovereign. God 'allowed' Satan to do it."
Contrary to the modern sovereignty teaching,
God is *not* in control of everything that happens to
you (again, see 1 John 5:19). Fatalism says that
God is responsible for everything that happens,
but the gospel declares that in all things God
works for the good of those who love him
(Romans 8:28). There is a difference. Jesus taught
us to pray, "Let your will be done on earth as it is
in heaven." Why would we need to pray that if
God's will was already being done?

7. When Doing Good is Bad for You

Ever since our ancestors ate the forbidden fruit, we humans have had an innate sense of good and evil. Help a blind person cross the street and *you just know* you're doing something good. Use a cat for a football and *you just know* you're doing something bad. You don't need anybody to tell you.

Knowing how to separate good from bad is a handy skill when buying apples or recruiting a baby-sitter. It's also the basis of every man-made religion under the sun. But your knowledge of good and evil does nothing to promote a life of dependency on Jesus.

Consider the person who treats the Bible as little more than an instruction manual for living. That is, they don't read it to grow in the knowledge of Jesus but to answer the question, "What good thing must I do to inherit eternal life?" Their line of thinking runs like this: *If I do good and avoid evil I will be judged to be a good person.* From a religious perspective, this makes perfect sense. It also explains why so many are asking, *What must I do?*

But there's a problem. In the Bible you will find some good things that are bad for you. Other things are good for one person but not for another. And then there are things that used to be good but aren't good any more. It's almost as if the Bible was designed to frustrate the religious quest for being good. It's almost as if the Author is trying to say, "Why do you ask me what is good? That's the wrong question."

The law is good...

The best example of something that is good yet bad for you is the law. Paul said the law is "holy, righteous, and good" (Romans 7:12). He also said, "the law is good if one uses it properly" (1 Timothy 1:8). When a moral person discovers the law their initial response is delight. "Finally, some good instructions to live by!" But when they try to keep the law they find themselves breaking it despite their best intentions. They try harder and fail again. Then the law — which is good — begins to condemn them (2 Corinthians 3:9). Worse, sin which they did not know they had until they met the law, rises up and begins to kill them (Romans 7:10–11).

Paul said the law is good but those who rely on it place themselves under a curse (Galatians 3:10). This seems paradoxical. How can something that is good be bad for us? Is the law defective? No — it's good! The problem is not with the law but your flesh. Your flesh cannot cope with the law (Romans 8:3). And it's not just the law. Anything that is good will become bad for you once your flesh gets involved: "For if you live according to the flesh you will die..." (Romans 8:13).

...but your flesh is weak

Every day the believer gets to choose between walking after the flesh or walking after the spirit. It's a mutually exclusive choice; it's one or the other. We walk after the flesh when we rely on our own resources — our resolve, our abilities, our understanding — and we walk after the spirit when we rely on his. It's the difference between walking by sight or by faith.

The problem is that walking after the flesh comes naturally to us. We've had a lot of practice. Before we were born of the Spirit the flesh was all we knew, and old habits die hard.

An illustration may help. I lived in Hong Kong for close to 15 years but now I live in New Zealand. Even though I am in New Zealand, I can still walk after the ways of Hong Kong — and to some extent I do. (I love Chinese New Year!)

The ways of Hong Kong are no better or worse than the ways of New Zealand, but the same cannot be said of the flesh. Walk after the flesh and your life will be barren and unprofitable: "It is the Spirit who gives life; the flesh profits nothing" (John 6:63, NKJV).

The supernatural and abundant life that we're called to live can only be received by faith and experienced when walking in the spirit. It's a choice we get to make. This is why the New Testament writers admonish us to put off the old ways of the flesh and put on the new ways of the spirit:

You were taught, with regard to your former way of life, to put off your old self, which is being corrupted by its deceitful desires; to be made new in the attitude of your minds; and to put on the new self, created to be like God in true righteousness and holiness. (Ephesians 4:22–24)

We don't put off and put on to *become* spiritual; we do it because we *are* spiritual. Everyone who is born again is born of the spirit. Since we are already in the spirit, let us walk after the spirit (Galatians 5:25).

The great religious blind spot

One of our biggest blind spots is we've bought into the idea that good things are good for us while bad things are bad for us. But this good versus evil logic is fruit off the wrong tree. It gets us keeping score in a game God isn't playing. The real issue is life versus death. And if you sow to the flesh you will reap corruption regardless of what you do.

"Wait a second Paul. Are you saying I can do no good walking after the flesh?" You can do a lot of good walking after the flesh, but it won't do *you* much good. "The flesh profits nothing." Live like this and you will be functionally identical to a moral atheist. You will miss opportunities to reveal the kingdom of God supernaturally. You will be acting like a "mere man" (see 1 Corinthians 3:3).

Jesus didn't suffer and die to make sinners good but to make the dead live. Christ is your life. When you walk after the flesh you are acting like the dead man you used to be. You are wasting your life in dead-end pursuits. You can spend all your days doing good works but none of it will result in praise to your heavenly Father because they are your works and not his. You may feel like you're making a mark but in reality you're just accumulating fuel for the fire.

Sadly, this is exactly how many Christians choose to live. Ask them to define the works of the flesh and they will recite Paul's list of manifest examples in Galatians 5. These are the biggies, if you like. It never occurs to them that walking after flesh can also bring death to the humdrum activity of everyday life, as the Bible describes elsewhere (e.g., through worry, serving God out of a sense of obligation, blaming others when things go wrong, etc.).

Do you see the dangers of walking after the flesh? Here's a simple test to find out: Which of the following gives you greater concern as a Christian?

1. Doing something bad in a moment of rash passion, or
2. Wasting my life doing my good works in the power of the flesh.

I suspect more people are fearful of doing something bad in a rash moment than they are of wasting their lives walking after the flesh. But a Christian who, in a momentary loss of sanity, fools around with sin, may be more likely to come to his senses than one who has been dulled by years of service done in the flesh. I am certainly not encouraging you to go out and do bad things. Nor am I trying to discourage you from doing good things. (Galatians 6:9 exhorts us not to grow weary of doing good.) What I am trying to do is show you that we can walk after the flesh regardless of what we do and even if we doing something good. When we walk after the old way of the flesh, what seems good and right to us now will eventually lead to death and disappointment.

It's time we discarded the forbidden fruit and got our nourishment from the Tree of Life which is Christ. Our innate tendency to judge ourselves as good or bad based on the good or bad things we are doing, is doing nobody any good at all.

A word after

"Paul, let me get this straight. Are you saying I can spend my life doing good works and have it all count for nothing? That I can actually do harm by doing good?" That is exactly what I'm saying. In fact, this is probably the oldest mistake in the book. When Adam and Eve ate the forbidden fruit, they thought they were doing something good.

The tree of knowledge of good and evil was not a bad tree; God doesn't do bad trees (Genesis 1:31). Everything in the world was good so the serpent had to tempt Eve with something that seemed "good and pleasing" to her (Genesis 3:6). It's an old trick that still works.

Most people think of themselves as good and decent people. Most aren't tempted to go out and do bad things but they are quick to do things that seem good at the time, and this is where the danger lies. The danger is not what they are doing, but what they are trusting. Adam and Eve trusted their own good judgment and got into serious trouble. So can we.

"Paul, can you give me some examples?" In this chapter we looked at one example of walking after the flesh in the pursuit of something good, namely, trying to keep the law. But there are plenty more, as we shall see in the next chapter...

8. How to Walk After the Flesh
In Twenty Easy Lessons

If you've ever taken young children to the zoo, you will know that the big animals tend to be more popular than the small ones. Elephants, rhinos, and tigers get more attention than otters, turtles, and geckos. And so it is with works of the flesh.

Ask any Christian to list the works of the flesh and they will likely respond with the list found in Galatians 5:19–21: adultery, hatred, idolatry, murder, etc. Paul calls these the manifest or obvious works of the flesh. They are the biggies, the elephantine examples of what it means to live apart from God. But the Bible also provides dozens of lesser examples that you may not be familiar with. I've listed some of these lesser works of the flesh below.

What does it mean to walk after the flesh? Walking after the flesh is when you attempt to get your needs met independently of God. It's trusting in yourself (your abilities, your understanding) and living solely from the basis of your earthly experience (what you see, hear, touch, etc.). Now here's something you may not know: You can walk after the flesh in the pursuit of both good things and bad things. Paul's manifest works of the flesh—the biggies—are all clearly associated with bad deeds, but some of the lesser works below are not bad at all. This is a critical point. We are not comparing good deeds with bad, but flesh with spirit. And when you're walking after the flesh even good things can be bad for you.

As we saw in the last chapter, a classic example of something that is good yet bad for you is God's law. It is not sin, it is good! But try to live by it and you will find yourself walking after the flesh every time. Paul said his ability to keep the righteous requirements of the law was ineffective because he tried to do so in the puny strength of his flesh (Romans 8:3). Living under self-imposed law is one of the main ways we walk after the flesh—hence its position at the top of my list.

Just a reminder: The wrong way to read this list is the carnal way—identifying things you should or should not do. We are less interested in the *what* than in the *how*. So how do we walk after the flesh? Here are twenty ways:

20 ways to walk after the flesh

1. Try to keep God's law (Romans 7:9–25): Think that you have to do stuff to be blessed and that you have to perform to stay saved.

2. Set your mind on earthly things (Philippians 3:19): Keep your eyes on the here and now. "What you see is all there is" (see Colossians 3:2). Entangle yourself in the affairs of life (2 Timothy 2:4).

3. Think about how to gratify the lusts of the flesh (Romans 13:14): If it feels good, do it.

4. Pursue your goal through self-denial (Colossians 2:21–23): Don't look, don't drink, don't touch. Fast twice a week. Worship perfectionism (Galatians 3:3, KJV).

5. Make sacrifices to impress God (Hebrews 10:8): Be conscious of your debt to Jesus and consider it your duty to serve him. Put your ministry or business before your marriage and family.

6. Load others with heavy burdens (Luke 11:46): Expect your Christian staff to work harder for less pay. Send the message that the work is more important than their families or health. Shackle them to your vision. Use emotional manipulation and scriptures to pressure people to support you.

7. Take pride in your independence (Jeremiah 17:5): Respect no one, scorn authority, flaunt your freedom. Say things like, "Who needs fathers? I follow Christ" (1 Corinthians 1:12).

8. Worry about your life (Matthew 6:25, Luke 8:14): "What shall we eat? What shall we drink? What shall we wear?" Entertain fear and doubt. "I can't do it" (Philippians 4:13).

9. Cultivate self-belief (2 Corinthians 12:10): "I can do it!" Boast in your accomplishments (2 Corinthians 11:30). Boast in your wisdom, strength and riches (Jeremiah 9:23).

10. See yourself as a victim (Romans 8:37): "Woe is me. I'm not worthy. My sinful nature made me do it." Blame God (James 1:13). Blame the devil (1 John 4:4). Blame your circumstances.

11. Be a man-pleaser (Galatians 1:10): Wonder, what will my boss think? How will the board react? How will this affect the tithers? Say only what they want you to say.

12. Make plans in a worldly manner (2 Corinthians 1:17): Do a SWOT analysis; list the pros and cons; make decisions based on money. Manage the risks and stay in control.

13. Try to grow a ministry (Psalm 127:1, 1 Corinthians 3:6). Work hard to make things happen.

14. Define success by human standards (1 Corinthians 1:26): It's all about the numbers. "How many soldiers do we have? How many attend the prayer meeting? Are donations increasing? Are we doing better than last year? Am I doing better than my predecessor or rival?"

15. Nurture your reputation (Philippians 3:8): Put on a good show and make a good impression (Galatians 6:12). Be face conscious. Make a name for yourself (Genesis 11:4) and blame the wife when things go wrong (Genesis 3:12).

16. Pray long prayers, especially if others are listening (Matthew 6:5–8).

17. Regard others from a worldly point of view (2 Corinthians 5:16): Engage in office politics. View new-comers as potential recruits for your programs. Cultivate task-based friendships. Choose the best-looking man for the job (1 Samuel 16:7). Show favor to the one with money (James 2:3–4).

18. Sacrifice people on the altar of your principles (1 Corinthians 3:3): "I'm right, you're wrong." Judge the weak (Romans 15:1). Distance yourselves from those who aren't as doctrinally pure as you (1 Corinthians 9:22).

19. Combat problems with worldly weapons (2 Corinthians 10:4): Put your faith in politics. Start fights (Zechariah 4:6). Picket the abortion clinic. Protest the gay parade (Isaiah 42:2).

20. Pretend to be Jesus (Matthew 24:24): Draw people to your ministry and build toward yourself (1 Thessalonians 3:8). Teach others to depend on you. Stand in the gap. Crucify yourself (Galatians 2:20).

This is a yukky list and frankly, I didn't enjoy writing it. Just about everything on this list, I've done. God help me, some of the things on this list I'm still doing!

Don't let this list condemn you. A better response is to get mad because we've been misled. We've been raised to believe that this is how things are done and that the fleshly way of life is normal. But this is *not* normal life for one born of the spirit.

Why do we walk after the flesh? Most of the time we do it out of habit and ignorance. We don't realize there's a better way. We walk after the flesh because when we were in the flesh this was how we lived: "You used to walk in these ways, in the life you once lived" (Colossians 3:7). The good news is that now we get to make a choice. We can choose to walk in the old way of the flesh or the new and better way of the spirit.

I have to say this again: Some of the activities on this list are good. Please don't think I am against the law or fruitful ministries or planning or praying without ceasing. I am not.

But understand that the natural mind longs to be told what to do when God is much more interested in how we are doing it. Are we trusting in the power of our might or are we resting confidently in his? Are we walking as we used to or are we being revealed as mature sons and daughters of our Father? Flesh cannot give birth to spirit. Neither can walking after the flesh empower you to live the life God has called you to live.

A word after

Trying to please God by keeping his law is a common way of walking after the flesh. However, I am more tempted to lean on the flesh in other ways; number twelve, for instance, the one about making plans in a worldly manner. I'm fairly sure I'm taking that scripture out of context, but the larger point stands — trusting in your own understanding is an inferior way to live (see Jeremiah 17:5).

I love to make plans. When I was a business school professor I taught people how to write business plans and do SWOT analyses. This sort of stuff comes easy to me. That's the problem. It's not hard for me to run ahead in my own strength and leave God entirely out of the equation.

After reading this article a lady who works in a Christian organization said to me, "We do SWOT analyses, set goals, and try to grow the ministry. It feels very business oriented, but it's *kingdom* business. And it has been successful with many people coming to Christ."

I told her that her story testifies to the goodness of God in drawing people to himself and I reminded her that there is nothing inherently wrong with planning and goal-setting. But being plan-led can get in the way of being spirit-led, especially if our plans are constrained by what we see and understand. This is a limited way to live.

The story of my life is this: I made a plan; God had a better one. I thought I could attain a certain level; God took me higher. This pattern has been repeated so frequently I often wonder if my best-laid plans are nothing more than set-ups for divine jokes, as though God was saying, "You thought you were going to accomplish *what* by *when*? That's funny!"

I have learned not to hold tightly to my plans and that when you walk after the spirit—when you are open to his gentle leading and direction—God will often take you places that were far better than you could imagine or conceive. My plans may be jokes, but the good news is that God's punch lines are awesome.

9. Seven Signs You Might Be Living Under Law

This week I finally got to see the movie, *The Book of Eli*. If you like stories where a lone man has to stand up to the wicked while trying to distribute the word of God in a post-apocalyptic world, then this is the movie for you. Just don't show it at your youth group. It is extremely violent. Still, it made me think about how people try to use God's word for nefarious purposes.

In the movie Eli carries the last known copy of the Bible. He comes to a town where Carnegie, the local strong man, has been trying to find a Bible. Eli's not about to give up the world's last Bible to a villain, so conflict ensues.

Mid-way through the story, one of Carnegie's thugs asks why they are being pushed so hard just to get a book. In an explosion of rage, Carnegie reveals his diabolical motive:

> It's not a book! It's a weapon. A weapon aimed right at the hearts and minds of the weak and the desperate. It will give us control of them. If we want to rule more than one small town, we have to have it. People will come from all over, they'll do exactly what I tell 'em if the words are from the book. It's happened before and it'll happen again. All we need is that book.[1]

---

[1] Albert Hughes and Allen Hughes (directors), *The Book of Eli*. 2010. Alcon Entertainment: USA.

There's a world of truth in that statement. The Bible is universally known as "the Good Book" and rightly so for it will point you to Jesus. Read the whole Bible through the lens of the cross and you will find redemption and life.

But when handled incorrectly the Bible is utterly lethal for buried within lies the law which, the Bible warns, ministers death (2 Corinthians 3:7). For thousands of years, men like Carnegie have been using the law-bits of the Bible to control and manipulate others. Their goal is to enslave and dominate and their tools are fear and condemnation.

People have been living under law ever since Adam and Eve ate from the tree of knowledge of good and evil. Jesus died to set us free from the curse of the law, yet some keep returning to the forbidden tree for another bite. To the degree that we are under law we have fallen from grace and are cut off from Christ (Galatians 5:4).

I'd like to think that if I'd been Adam, I would've built a fence around that tree. Then I would've put warning signs all over that fence. It's too late for that now, but it's not too late to put warning signs around the law. Below is the beginnings of a list of signs that reveal whether you are living under the enslaving yoke of law or walking free in God's divine grace. My purpose in making this list is not to condemn you, but to see you standing firm and free in Christ!

1. You're not 100% sure if you're 100% forgiven

God doesn't do forgiveness in installments. All your sins were forgiven at the cross when God the Son abolished sin by the sacrifice of himself (Hebrews 9:26).

Neither God the Father nor God the Holy Spirit remembers your sin any more (Hebrews 8:12, 10:17). In Christ, you are completely and eternally forgiven (Colossians 2:13).

2. You believe you have a duty or responsibility to serve the Lord

Duty and responsibility are synonyms for obligation so this is a mindset that says you are obliged, or indebted, to God. Perhaps you have heard it said that "Jesus has done so much for you, what will you do for him?" Indeed, God has given us everything and he did it so that "he might show the incomparable riches of his grace, expressed in his kindness to us in Christ Jesus" (Ephesians 2:7). He is not just rich in grace, but exceedingly rich.

We cheapen his grace by thinking we have a responsibility to pay him back. Our responsibility is to believe that he is good and true! It is not our obligation to serve the Lord, it is our royal privilege. It is not our duty, but our great delight.

3. You suffer from performance anxiety

Performance anxiety is a natural response to the uncertainty of life under the old covenant, but anxiety has no place in the new. We are to draw from the wells of salvation with joy (Isaiah 12:3). Those under law will battle anxiety and fear, but those under grace walk with joy and thanksgiving.

> Happy are those whose wrongs are forgiven, whose sins are pardoned! Happy is the person whose sins the Lord will not keep account of! (Romans 4:7–8, GNB)

God has made us his sons, and with such a Father we need not be worried about anything (Matthew 6:32). He is our Provider who delights to give good gifts to those who ask him (Matthew 7:11). Those who serve under the law are insecure, but sons are secure.

4. You think, "God will bless me as I do my part"

The essence of a life enslaved by law is the mindset that says, "I must do something for God." The motivation may be to earn salvation or some other blessing, but this mindset is anti-Christ and anti-cross. We are not justified by what we do but by grace alone (Romans 3:24). Grace and works don't mix (Romans 11:6). Grace, peace, and every spiritual blessing have

been given to us by God our Father through Jesus
Christ (Ephesians 1:3).

5. You think we need more preaching on repentance

Repentance saves lives, but preaching on repentance
doesn't lead to repentance. A law mindset emphasizes what people must do (repent!), but grace
proclaims what God has already done (everything!).
A law mindset uses inferior incentives (e.g., fear and
judgment) that lead to temporary changes in behavior,
but grace (God is good and he loves you!) changes the
hardest heart.

If you want people to genuinely repent, preach
the goodness of God (Romans 2:4).

6. You think you have to overcome life's trials or Jesus will blot out your name

This really isn't about you for Jesus is our overcomer
and victory (John 16:33). If you believe he is the Son
of God you have already overcome the world,
because the Overcomer lives in you (1 John 5:4–5).

Jesus promised the overcomers at Sardis that he
would never blot out their name. Since then insecure
performance-oriented believers have feared he might
change his mind and do exactly that.

He won't.

7. You mainly think of following Jesus in terms of giving up things

Christianity is a divine exchange, our life for his. No doubt you've heard people say that following Jesus costs you everything and it does. You cannot call him Lord without renouncing the right to your own life. But see what you get in exchange! If salvation means nothing more to you than self-denial and personal sacrifice, you've missed the whole point. Christ offers us an unfair exchange; *our life for his*. God favors us with this exchange. We give him our sinful selves and get everything in return. A law mindset looks at what we give up, but a grace mindset rejoices at what he offers in return! Stop thinking about what you gave up (nothing you could keep) and start enjoying what he has given you (everything!).

A word after

Some people doodle, I write lists. One day I felt inspired to list all the ways that we can put ourselves under law. By the end of the day I had listed 93 different ways! I took the first seven points on my list and put them in the article you see above.

When the article came out, number five ("You think we need more preaching on repentance") got the biggest reaction. At the time I didn't realize that repentance is a touchy subject. But I soon learned…

10. Why Repentance is like Football

What comes to mind when you hear the word football? Your answer to that question says a lot about where you come from. If you're a fan of football and you travel the world you may have conversations like this:

"So you like footy. Who's your favorite team?"
"Collingwood."
"Never heard of them. Do they play in the Bundesliga?"
"The Bundes-what-now?"

It's a bit like that with the word repentance. Here on E2R there has been a lot of discussion regarding the purpose of repentance. Much of that discussion is like the conversation above. We're all fans of repentance but we seem to be talking about different things.

So what is repentance?

Like football, your answer to that question says a lot about where you're coming from. If you've been raised under rule-based religion, repentance is *something we must do to be saved*. If you don't repent, you're not saved.

What is the *something* we must we do? Turn from sin of course. It's resolving to not break the rules. But this is a limited and misleading interpretation of repentance.

What is repentance?

The New Testament words for repent and repentance are derived from the Greek word for mind. To repent is to change your mind. Nothing more, nothing less. Let's look at an example from scripture:

> "The time has come," he said. "The kingdom of God has come near. Repent and believe the good news!" (Mark 1:15)

This is where the football confusion starts to kick in. The rule-focused mind interprets Jesus' words as "turn from sin and believe the good news." But Jesus is addressing unbelievers, not rule-breakers. He's talking to those who have never heard about the kingdom of God. He is saying "change your unbelieving mind and believe the good news."

Repentance is not primarily a sin issue, it's a faith issue. In the old covenant, repentance meant saying no to sin; in the new it means saying yes to Jesus.

Now that we know the essence of repentance (a change of mind), I want to address three common myths or misconceptions.

Myth 1: Repentance compels God to forgive me

> … repentance and forgiveness of sins will be preached in his name to all nations, beginning at Jerusalem. (Luke 24:47)

The one who is inclined towards self-improvement reads this and thinks "I need to repent to get forgiven." In other words, God will not forgive me unless I do something. This is pure hubris. It's straight out of the old covenant. God is God and he does not need your permission to forgive you.

We don't repent to get forgiven; we repent because we are forgiven. This is the good news! You need to repent and believe it. Repentance doesn't make God forgive you; it helps you receive by faith the gift of forgiveness that has been made available in Christ Jesus.

Myth 2: Repentance means turning from sin

Since repentance means changing your mind, it's certainly possible that one can repent by turning from sin and there are plenty of people in the Bible who did so. But that is only one kind of repentance and it is not the kind that leads to salvation. In the New Testament, repentance typically means turning to God.

> I have declared to both Jews and Greeks that they must *turn to God in repentance* and have faith in our Lord Jesus. (Act 20:21, emphasis added)

Turning from versus *turning to* may seem like splitting hairs, but it's the difference between life and death. Someone who turns to God automatically turns from sin and dead works, but someone who turns from sin does not automatically turn to God. This is why it is misleading to preach repentance as turning from sin. Paul never did. "I preached that they should repent and turn to God" (Act 26:20).

If you want to understand the difference between turning from and turning to, consider the Pharisees. They ran away anytime sin appeared. If anyone knew how to turn from sin they did, yet Jesus called them sons of hell (Matthew 23:15). Turning from sin might make you a moral person, but it won't make you righteous.

Jesus said if you want to enter the kingdom of heaven, you need to be more righteous than the self-righteous Pharisees (Matthew 5:20). Righteousness, like forgiveness, comes to us as a gift. It is received through faith in Christ alone. If you don't believe that then you need to repent and turn to God who makes us righteous.

Myth 3: Repentance means feeling sorry for sin

According to some repentance is not genuine unless there are tears involved. It is not enough that you turn to God, you also need to produce remorse, regret, and feelings of guilt. Fail to manufacture these emotions and your repentance is suspect. You've not really repented. So you'd better go away, ponder your sins some more, and come back when you're ready to have a good cry about them.

This is pure emotionalism. This is old covenant sackcloth and ashes. This is Judas killing himself with grief. The good news is supposed to release great joy, not great sorrow. When you've heard that God loves you and has forgiven you and provided everything you need for life and godliness, why would you be sad?

There may indeed be sorrow involved when you realize that you have missed the way and wasted your life, but it's only godly sorrow if it leads you to God. Godly sorrow and repentance go together, but it's unlikely that you will cry every time you change your mind about the Lord. In truth, it doesn't really matter how your emotions respond when you learn about God's goodness. It only matters that you believe it.

Repentance, like football, means different things to different people. But only one code of the game is played in heaven (it's rugby, of course). Similarly, there's only one kind of repentance that matters to God and that's the kind that leads you to him. His heart's desire is for you to come to him. You can come happy or come sad but the main thing is that you come.

A word after

If social security is the third rail of politics, then repentance must be the third rail of Christianity. Like social security, everyone agrees that repentance is a good thing, but people differ on what form it should take and how much is needed.

This article attracted many comments that demonstrated the point I was trying to make — that repentance means different things to different people. In settings where the rules are esteemed above people, and sin is defined as rule-breaking, repentance usually implies punishment. It's the big stick you get for disobedience. The problem with this approach is it doesn't work. It leaves unaddressed the heart issue that led to the mistake in the first place.

True repentance, in contrast, implies an opportunity for genuine restoration and healing. True repentance, has nothing to do with punishment, which drives us apart, but love, which draws us together.

Repentance is not something we do in response to sin; it's something we do in response to love.

11. Why Confession is Still Good for You

If you know me, you will know that nothing winds me up faster than telling people they must do things like confess to be forgiven. I've said it before and I'll say it again, confessing your sins does not compel God to forgive you. God does not forgive us on account of our confession but in accordance with his grace.

Since I bang this drum loudly and often, some have concluded that I am opposed to confession. Nothing could be further from the truth. As I have said from the beginning, confession is good for you. Or rather, confession can be good for you — if it's done properly.

In the pursuit of self-righteousness, confession is a hideous thing. It is introspective navel-gazing that promotes sin- and self-consciousness. Among Catholics and Protestants alike, confession of sins is sometimes sold as the price you must pay to receive the gift of forgiveness. To enjoy God's grace and fellowship we're told to admit our crimes, no matter how small. To the natural mind this seems like a good deal; you talk, you walk. But it is a prostitution of a great and priceless love.

Let's be clear — either the love of God is uncon-ditional or it's not love. Unless you receive his for-giveness as a free gift you won't receive it at all.

There is no doubt that the practice of confession has been abused, but as a friend of mine likes to say, the correct response to abuse is not non-use but proper use. So what is the proper use of confession and why should we do it? Let me suggest two good reasons for confession:

1. Confession helps us to receive grace

Grace is not for everyone, only the needy. To receive God's grace, we must first acknowledge our need for grace. Paul said, "My God shall supply all your need…" (Philippians 4:19). If you don't recognize your need, you won't receive his supply.

This point is often lost among those of us who proclaim grace. We preach that "you are as righteous, holy, and perfect as Jesus" — and we are right to do so. In Christ you are all those things.

But what if there is a disconnect between your identity and experience? You may say, "I know I am righteous but I don't *feel* righteous. I'm battling with unrighteous thoughts." You've got two choices: You can pretend that there's no problem or you can come to the throne of grace to receive grace in your hour of need.

Let me give you an example. A few years I was battling a certain temptation that just wouldn't go away. I had done nothing wrong, but I was vulnerable. I was heading in a bad direction and felt powerless to stop.

So what did I do? I confessed my need for grace. I prayed the best prayer a needy man can pray: "God, help!" I cast my anxieties upon him and he helped me.

Within a day the stronghold was broken and I was completely free. The temptation no longer had any hold on me. That's how grace works. God gives grace to the humble — to those who are honest and open about their needs and weaknesses — and his grace changes us.

In this case I confessed my need and was set free by grace. But what if things had gotten worse and I had fallen into sin? What then? Again, confession can help but not for the reasons usually taught. Remember, confession doesn't manipulate God into forgiving us. So what good is confession when we sin?

2. Confession helps me to live whole

One of the ways sin hurts us is through guilt and condemnation. Guilt is a sign that something is wrong and needs to be addressed; confession is a good way to address it.

> When I kept silent, my bones wasted away through my groaning all day long… my strength was sapped as in the heat of summer. Then I acknowledged my sin to you and did not cover up my iniquity. I said, "I will confess my transgressions to the Lord." (Psalm 32:3–5)

I hear from people all the time who are torn up inside on account of some past sin. They may have some understanding of God's grace and they may even accept that they are forgiven, yet they still battle with guilt. It's as if there is this sin parasite inside them, eating them alive. Like David, their bones are wasting away and their strength is sapped.

If this is you, drag that dark thing into the light. Talk to your heavenly Father about it or find a trusted friend. Sin thrives in darkness and we are called to be children of the light.

David suffered because he kept silent. Here's the equation: Sin + silence = suffering. This is the maths of Adam that leads us to hide behind bushes of blame and facades of self-righteousness. Now let me show you the new math of Jesus: Sin + confession = healing. Here's the relevant scripture:

> Make this your common practice: Confess your sins to each other and pray for each other so that you can live together whole and healed. (James 5:16, MSG)

Sin is utterly destructive and we mustn't pretend otherwise. But just as sunshine kills germs, the light of God's grace breaks the power of sin and darkness.

As a church leader, James understood this. He knew that one of the ways we receive God's grace is through our grace-giving brothers and sisters. James was not trying to shackle you with an accountability partner; he was giving you wisdom on how to live free.

Quit pretending and 'fess up

Sin has power over us whenever we try to resist it in our own strength. If you're thinking, "I'm okay, I can handle this, I can't let anyone know I'm struggling," then beware the slippery slope! God resists the proud, but gives grace to the humble. Want grace? Then admit your need for it.

To recap: Confessing our sins does not compel God to forgive us. (He already did.) Neither does confession restore fellowship with an offended Father. (He promised to never leave nor forsake us.) Confession, or freely acknowledging our needs and total dependence on God, is our faith-filled response to God our Helper. Confession helps us walk in the supernatural power of his grace.

A word after

I said earlier that it's helpful to draw dividing lines separating grace from mixture, but sometimes those lines get confused. For instance, there is a perception that grace preachers are preaching a law of "Thou shalt not confess!" As I explain in my book *The Hyper-Grace Gospel*, this is a myth. We are not against confession; we are for confession as the Bible defines it.

Biblical confession is essential for receiving grace (see Romans 10:9–13, Philippians 4:19). However, ritualistic confession done in the hope of earning God's gifts, is dangerous. How do you tell the difference? Biblical confession will always leave you focused on Jesus and his goodness, while ritualistic confession will leave you focused on yourself and your shortcomings. The former is always Son-conscious, while the latter is sin-conscious.

Proverbs 28:13 says, "Whoever conceals their sins does not prosper, but the one who confesses and renounces them finds mercy." Confessing sins doesn't compel God to forgive you, but it certainly helps you to find or receive the grace he has given us through his Son. This is a truth to be believed before it is felt. As I say in *The Hyper-Grace Gospel*:

> When you sin it takes no faith to beat yourself up and agree with the Accuser who calls you a sinner. It takes faith to look at the cross and say, "Thank you, Jesus, for carrying all my sin." It takes faith to praise your Father for his superabounding grace that is greater than your transgression. And it takes faith to agree with the Holy Spirit who says, despite what you did, you are still righteous, acceptable, and pleasing to God.

12. Where was God in the Connecticut School Shooting?

Yet another school shooting has resulted in the loss of innocent lives and now questions are being asked: "Where was God? Why didn't God stop this? Why didn't God protect the lives of those twenty children and six staff members?"

For a grieving parent, these are normal questions. When you have suffered the greatest loss any human can suffer it is perfectly understandable to scream, *Why?* Death is awful. It is an enemy. I hate it and God hates it too.

I hesitate to write because many are using this latest tragedy as an opportunity to grandstand and advance their particular causes. "We need fewer guns. We need more prayer. We need to turn back to God and stop abortions."

Causes have their place but in a week when families are burying their children, this is not the time. But the questions aren't going away. Loud men with agendas are shouting at us. "God is judging America! We need to repent! We need to legislate the kingdom of God into existence!"

How should we respond to these loud men?

I usually respond to foolishness by ignoring it. But this morning someone "new to the grace teaching" wrote to me and asked for my thoughts. Here they are:

1. Is God judging America?

No. Anyone who tells you otherwise is unacquainted with the gospel. The sins of America, along with the sins of every other nation, were judged at the cross. If Christ's death was a sufficient sacrifice — and it was (see Hebrews 10:12) — then God cannot judge America for her sins. It would be unjust for God to judge the same sin twice.

When an earthquake flattened my hometown in 2011, some said God was judging Christchurch for its sins. By that logic God should have wiped America off the face of the map because the sins of a city are few in comparison to the sins of a superpower. I'll say now what I said then: The cross — not earthquakes or massacres — is God's remedy for sin.

The sins of America were forgiven or done away with long before the Mayflower Pilgrims landed at Plymouth Rock. Sin certainly has destructive consequences, as we have just seen in Connecticut, but divine judgment is not one of them. Jesus is the Prince of Peace.

2. Whose fault was it?

Not God's. "The highest heavens belong to the Lord, but the earth he has given to man" (Psalm 115:16).

God gave us this planet and we are responsible for much of what happens. Who first sinned and opened the door to death? It wasn't God. It was one of us (Roman 5:12).

Some are now saying that we let Satan into our schools when we took the prayer out. Actually, Satan's been messing with us a lot longer than that. His evil influence goes all the way back to the Garden. But Satan could not have influenced us if we had not listened to his lies.

The blame game isn't helpful, but if you must point the finger, blame Adam whose decision to reject God brought death to us all, or blame his offspring who built a civilization on violence. But don't blame God. That's like blaming the sun for the darkness.

3. What did we do to deserve this?

Nothing. When bad things happen we tend to wonder, "What did I do to deserve this?" This is the voice of religious reason. It's Job sitting in the ashes examining his navel for unconfessed sin. "I'm pretty sure I've been good, yet I've lost everything so maybe I wasn't."

We are natural scorekeepers. When good things happen we tell ourselves it's because we've been good. So when bad things happen we must've been bad. Some call it karma but like all manmade religion it is fruit off the wrong tree.

Two thousand years ago a tower collapsed killing eighteen people. This tragedy led Jesus to pose a question to the religious-minded folk of his day, "Do you think that those who died were more sinful than all the others living in Jerusalem? I tell you, no!" (Luke 13:4–5).

Sometimes people die because they are in the wrong place at the wrong time. Had those children and teachers at Sandy Hook done anything deserving of death? Of course not. There may be no lesson here. No "avoid this next time." All we can take from this, said Jesus, is that death comes to us all. So repent, and come to him for new life (Luke 13:5).

4. Why didn't God stop this from happening?

In a manner of speaking, he couldn't—not without violating us. I know this will come as something of a shock, but God doesn't always get what he wants. He is not willing that any perish, yet people perish. God could intervene but he restrains himself on account of love.

Consider: The greatest massacre in history happened when Adam ate the forbidden fruit. Adam's act condemned the human race to death and God did nothing to stop it. It wasn't God's will for Adam to eat, yet Adam ate. And it wasn't God's will for Adam Lanza to go to that school in Connecticut , yet Adam went.

Free will is a powerful thing. With it we can choose life or death and Almighty God won't stop us. In giving us the freedom to choose knowing that he would have to go to the cross to redeem our choices,

God was saying that he would rather die than live without us.

5. Has God left the building?

No. The question, "Where was God?" implies that God is not here. Perhaps he skipped town when we stopped prayer in schools or when the Supreme Court decided Roe vs. Wade. "We're sinners and God doesn't want anything to do with us." Such thinking usually leads to a long list of *things we must do* to fix the problem.

What a deception! God did not leave us; we left him. God didn't reject Adam; Adam rejected God. "Adam, where are you?" (Genesis 3:9).

The story of our species is one of unrequited love. God made us for love but we spurned him. Since then he has waited for the prodigal to come to his senses and return home.

6. How should we respond?

With love and grace. This tragedy in Connecticut did not happen because God stopped loving us or caring for us. Neither did it happen because our religious performance is not what it could be. It happened because a certain young man made an awful choice and did a terrible thing.

What should we do in response? We should weep with those who weep and mourn with those who mourn. We should ache and hurt and cry because we live in a world where children sometimes die from bullets, poverty, and disease. We should pray for the families of Charlotte Bacon, Daniel Barden, Rachel D'Avino, Olivia Engel, Josephine Gay, Dylan Hockley, Dawn Lafferty Hochsprung, Madeleine Hsu, Catherine Hubbard, Chase Kowalski, Nancy Lanza, Jesse Lewis, Ana Marquez-Greene, James Mattioli, Grace McDonnell, Anne Marie Murphy, Emilie Parker, Jack Pinto, Noah Pozner, Caroline Previdi, Jessica Rekos, Avielle Richman, Lauren Rousseau, Mary Sherlach, Victoria Soto, Benjamin Wheeler, and Allison Wyatt. We could pray that in this dark night they might somehow know the comfort of God.

And when the time of mourning has passed we should get up and carry on with the task Jesus has given us — that of proclaiming the good news of his kingdom. We should provide a broken world with a prophetic picture of the age to come — the age where justice reigns and heaven and earth are one. Darkness only persists because the light does not shine, so shine.

The answer to violence is not to stick the Ten Commandments back in the courthouses or build higher walls around communities. For the children of God, these are inferior choices. What this sick and dying world needs most is a revelation of *God with us*.

God is not opposed to us. He loves us warts and all. While we were sinners he died for us and now he lives for us. What America and every other nation needs is a revelation of God's limitless love. They need to see Jesus.

A word after

Some days I get up and find my whole day is mapped out for me by E2R readers. In December 2012, I received the following message from a lady called Pat:

> I would be curious to hear your thoughts on the recent school tragedy in Connecticut. Specifically, where was God? The popular response to the question is that we have asked him to leave our institutional systems like government, education, and so on. That doesn't sit well with me, but I'm still new to the grace teaching, and would like to hear your thoughts.

I'm not usually able to respond to requests — there are so many of them — but something about this question stirred me to write. So if you liked the article above, you can thank Pat.

After it came out a mother of school-age children asked me this follow-up question: "If God can't stop violent acts from happening, why bother praying for protection?" To clarify, God certainly can stop things from happening. My point was that he didn't stop the Connecticut School shooting from happening. How do I know? Because it happened.

The mom who asked this question then shared the following story:

> When my daughter was in the 9th grade a boy was found in her school with a gun. He had a list on him and my child's name was on that list. Every day since then I've prayed for the Lord to protect my kids and their schools from shootings. I'm not saying that my prayers alone stopped this (maybe they did, I don't know) but all I know is that someone wanted to kill my child and they were stopped.

And thank God they were! But what lesson do we take from this?

If you are worried about your kids have the freedom to cast your cares upon the Lord. "Cast all your anxiety on him because he cares for you" (1 Peter 5:7). But don't fall for the lie that your prayers are the only thing protecting your children or that God won't intervene unless you pray. Job felt this way and his fears made him a superstitious man. Every time his kids went partying he felt like he had to offer sacrifices in case they'd sinned (Job 1:5). This is a fearful and faithless way to live.

Fear for our children can be a form of bondage. At some point we need to come to a place of restful trust in the Lord. We have to choose to believe that he cares for our kids even more than we do. It's not easy.

The world is a dangerous place and our children are small. We have to strive to enter his rest and one way to do that is to stand on his many wonderful promises to us (e.g., Isaiah 49:25, 54:13, Proverbs 12:7).

If I felt that my kids weren't safe *unless* I prayed for their protection, I'd never stop praying. I wouldn't have a life. But I choose to believe God's word. Now when one of them goes out I'm likely to pray, "Thank you, Father that you are watching over my kids even when I'm not. Thank you that you protect them even when I can't. Thank you that you care even when I forget to pray."

I don't beg God to do what he's promised to do. Instead I remind myself of his word and thank him for it. Job's fear made him superstitious but God's word can set you free. It's a totally different way to live.

13. Shipwrecked Faith

Timothy, my son, I am giving you this command
in keeping with the prophecies once made about
you, so that by recalling them you may fight the
battle well, holding on to faith and a good conscience, which some have rejected and so have
suffered shipwreck with regard to the faith.
Among them are Hymenaeus and Alexander,
whom I have handed over to Satan to be taught
not to blaspheme. (1 Timothy 1:18–20)

What does it mean to shipwreck your faith? Paul said
this had happened to at least two people so I guess it
can happen to you. But how does it happen and what
are the consequences? Most people have no idea but
fear the worst: "Shipwrecked faith means you've lost
your salvation. It means you're going to hell."

Actually, it means no such thing.

Look again at the passage above and note how
Paul defines fighting the good fight as "holding on to
faith and a good conscience." These two things are
connected. If you reject or cast away a good conscience your faith will become shipwrecked:

Holding fast to faith (that leaning of the entire
human personality on God in absolute trust and
confidence) and having a good (clear) conscience.
By rejecting and thrusting from them [their

85

conscience], some individuals have made shipwreck of their faith. (1 Timothy 1:19, AMP)

This is not about ignoring your conscience; it's about the dangers of thrusting away your *clear* conscience. In other words, if your conscience condemns you, you will have trouble believing what God says is true about you.

Dear friends, if our hearts do not condemn us, we have confidence before God and receive from him anything we ask... (1 John 3:21–22a)

Condemnation is a faith-killer. Condemnation will cause you to be timid before God making it hard for you to receive from the abundance of his grace. If your conscience is constantly telling you that you're unworthy, you're a hopeless Christian, and you don't deserve to be in the kingdom, you will be in danger of shipwrecking your faith.

What is shipwrecked faith?

If you are not secure in your Father's love — which you won't be if your conscience condemns you — you'll make a wreck of your faith. Like a ship that fails to reach its destination, you'll fall short of all that God has in store for you.

And no, that doesn't mean you'll lose your salvation and go to hell. It simply means you won't mature in the faith (Luke 8:14). You'll lose the freedom that is yours in Christ (Galatians 5:1) and you'll fear punishment that isn't coming (1 John 4:18).

The New Testament writers list many bad things that can happen when we fail to trust God in our daily lives, but the thing many Christians fear most — Christ writing them off — is the one thing that absolutely cannot happen. If you are one with the Lord be at peace, for the One who took hold of you will never let you go. If the Holy Spirit dwells in you he will never leave. Jesus promised (see John 14:16).

So what does it mean to shipwreck your faith? It means moving from the secure foundation of Jesus Christ. It means diluting your faith in God with faith in self, faith in effort, faith in your ability to perform. It's trying instead of trusting and striving instead of resting.

What Paul never said

"If you shipwreck your faith, you'll lose your salvation." Preachers of insecurity love to quote this verse as support for the idea that we can undo what we never wrought — as though we could unfuse the Holy Spirit from our spirits and tear ourselves from God's mighty grip. Don't you think if that could happen, Paul would've mentioned it? Yet he says nothing of the kind.

What Paul *does* say is that a group of certain men had shipwrecked their faith and of that group two men had been handed over to Satan so that they might be taught not to blaspheme. I don't know exactly what Paul had in mind with this handing over business — perhaps it meant kicking them out of the fellowship — but note that he did it with the intention of teaching them, not condemning them.

What else do we know about these two guys Paul handed over to Satan? We know they were part of a group of teachers (i) who were promoting controversies rather than God's work — which is by faith (v.4) and (ii) they saw themselves as teachers of the law (v.7).

Ask the right questions and you will get the right answers:

- How do we preach law? By telling people they must work for salvation/sanctification/blessings, and so on.
- What is the purpose of the law? Its purpose is to condemn us.
- What had happened to these law-teachers? Their consciences began to condemn them.
- What was the result of their ministry? God's finished work was no longer preached and their faith was shipwrecked.

Here's the story as I see it. After Paul left Ephesus, certain teachers arose from among their own number and began preaching law. They might have been

Judaizers with circumcision knives or they might have even preached the commands of Jesus. The point is not what sort of law they were preaching, but their improper application of it.

Paul said "the law is good if one uses it properly (but) they do not know what they are talking about or what they so confidently affirm" (vv.7–8). In any case, the outcome was they were distracting themselves and their hearers from "God's work—which is by faith" (v.4).

Paul said Hymenaeus and Alexander were blasphemers. To blaspheme is to slander or speak falsely of someone. It's saying things like; "The blood of Jesus doesn't avail for me." (It does!) "Jesus needs my help." (He doesn't!) "The Holy Spirit is convicting me of sin." (He isn't!) "God will not finish what he begun." (He will!) "I can sin my way out of his grace." (You can't!) This sort of teaching promotes controversy and distracts people from trusting in God's finished work.

Fight the good fight

I hope you understand that when it comes to saving you and making you acceptable to God, Jesus does it all and his perfect work cannot be improved upon. This is the gospel truth and it is worth fighting for. I am not talking about fighting people but demolishing arguments and taking captive every thought that is opposed to Christ. Usually this is a battle waged inside our own minds.

If your conscience condemns you as a sinner (Christ died for sinners!) or unworthy of grace (grace is for the unworthy!), the remedy is not to try and clean yourself and make yourself acceptable. That way lies disaster and shipwreck. The only cure for a guilty conscience is the cleansing blood of Jesus (Hebrews 10:22). It is seeing the cross and the empty tomb, and believing the good news that Jesus has done it all!

If someone uses the mirror of the law to point out your imperfections, don't cast off your good conscience but fix your eyes on Jesus and his glorious perfections. You are one with the Lord and as he is so are you in this world (1 John 4:17).

And the next time someone says, "You're not good enough for God and you need to work to improve yourself," tell them, "I am one with Christ and *he* is good enough for God, *his* work is finished, and in *him* I have found my eternal rest!"

A word after

I have nothing profound to add to this stunningly brilliant article (cough), so here's a shipwreck joke for you. (It's a classic!)

A tramp steamer is passing through the South Pacific when its crew observes smoke rising from what was thought to be an uninhabited island. The captain of the steamer decides to investigate and sets off in the longboat. He lands on the island and is greeted by a haggard man.

"I'm so glad you found me," says the man. "My boat was wrecked years ago and I have been stuck here alone ever since."

The captain asks, "If you're alone, how come I can see three huts?"

The survivor replies, "That one is my home and the other one is where I go to church."

"What about the third hut?" asks the captain.

The man replies with a scowl. "That's where I used to go to church."

14. What Happens to Christians Who Commit Suicide?

What do you say to the parents of a Christian teen-ager who has killed himself? I faced this situation several years ago and, I have tell you, it's not easy. Premature death is hard to handle at any time, but suicide leaves loved ones especially bewildered at its senselessness.

It seems the subject of suicide is a touchy one that Christians don't like to talk about. That's probably because most of us don't have anything good to say! Ask a believer, "What happens to Christians who kill themselves?" and you'll likely get one of the following responses:

1. They go to hell because they never repented for the sin of murder.
2. It's not up to us to judge — we don't know what happens.
3. It's a grave sin but God will somehow take care of it in his mysterious ways.

None of these responses brings much comfort to those who are left behind. But happily none of these responses is true. Let's compare each response with what the Bible says.

What does the Bible say about those who commit suicide?

First, do people who commit suicide go to hell? Not if they're saved. Revelations 21:8 tells us that the lake of fire — whatever that is — will be full of murderers. But you don't end up in the lake of fire *because* you are a murderer (see Revelation 20:15). If murder sent you to hell, King David would be a goner. But it doesn't and he isn't.

But didn't God say, "Thou shalt not murder"? He did — it's the sixth commandment and part of the law. There are harsh consequences for breaking the law but you are not under the law (Romans 6:14). When Jesus went to the cross he fulfilled the requirements of the law on your behalf so that you might live free from its curse. Don't look to your own obedience for salvation; look to his. On the cross Jesus carried the sins of the world and as a result you are completely and eternally forgiven.

But what about repentance? Don't we have to repent in order to receive forgiveness? Isn't this the stumbling block for those who kill themselves — that they never repent? No. We are not forgiven on the basis of anything we do or don't do. We are forgiven because of what Jesus has done. "In him we have the forgiveness of sins" (Ephesians 1:7).

In God's eyes you are forgiven whether you repent or don't repent. To say, you must repent to be forgiven, is to cheapen the riches of his grace. The blood of Jesus paid for the sins of the whole world, including the unrepentant and suicidal (1 John 2:2).

This isn't to say that all are saved, for we all need to respond to the grace of God by faith (Ephesians 2:8). Everyone is forgiven but not everyone has received the gift of his righteousness (Romans 1:17). But we are talking here about those who are saved when they die. Can a Christian nullify God's forgiveness by committing suicide? No, it's impossible. God's gifts are irrevocable.

Second, to say, "we don't know what happens to Christians who kill themselves" reveals an ignorance of God's promises. We *do* know what happens: They go to be with Jesus (John 14:3). Some say that "suicide is a grave sin," but is there any sin that's not?

The good news is that God's grace is greater than our gravest sins. His best is better than our worst (Romans 5:20). Just as we are not qualified by our good deeds, neither are we disqualified by our bad. We were condemned by Adam's disobedience but now we have been justified through Christ's obedience:

> So then, just as sin ruled by means of death, so also God's grace rules by means of righteousness, leading us to eternal life through Jesus Christ our Lord. (Romans 5:21, GNB)

Third, to offer vague comfort by saying, "God will take care of it in some mysterious way," is to insult the finished work of the cross. Take care of it? He already did! He came and died and rose again so that in him we might have resurrection life:

> I am the resurrection and the life. The one who believes in me will live, even though they die. (John 11:25)

Look closely at this promise of Jesus and see if you can find any conditions pertaining to the means of death. There are none! The way in which you shrug off your earthsuit has absolutely no bearing on his promise of resurrection life. Whether you die in a house fire, from an over-dose, or go down with the Titanic, the one who believes in Jesus will live, even though he dies.

The main thing

For those who are left behind, suicide hits like a Mack truck. But allow me to bring some perspective to this issue.

The single most important fact of your life is not where you were born or how you die, but whether you are in Christ—whether you have put your trust in him and confessed him as Lord.

You can be born a prince and die on a field of glory, but unless you know Jesus it's all for naught. Conversely, you can die a nobody but if Jesus knows you all is eternally well. If you have lost someone to suicide and they belonged to Jesus all is not lost. You will be with them again. Believe what God has promised and don't let anyone tell you otherwise.

It is beyond the scope of this article to discuss those things that might drive a believer to suicide. Perhaps you find it inconceivable that someone acquainted with the goodness of God would ever consider ending their lives. But only God knows the depth of pain that some of our brothers and sisters have to endure in this world.

The teenager I mentioned above took his own life because he was the ongoing victim of a sexual predator and he could see no other way out. Who am I to say that I would've chosen differently if I had been in his shoes? I'm not trying to justify suicide. I'm saying I can't condemn those who, for reasons I cannot fathom, prefer death to life.

It's too late to help that young man but it's not too late to comfort his parents and those of who have lost loved ones. Maybe you have heard words of condemnation or hollow comfort. Maybe you've been be told that the one you lost is lost for eternity. If so, I encourage you to find rest in the grace of our loving Father and to cultivate the same conviction as Paul:

> For I am convinced that neither death nor life, neither angels nor demons, neither the present nor the future, nor any powers, neither height nor depth, nor anything else in all creation, will be able to separate us from the love of God that is in Christ Jesus our Lord. (Romans 8:38–9)

A *word after*

I wrote this article with a specific family in mind and I have been pleased to see that it has since brought a measure of comfort to other families in similar situations. I'm talking about families who have lost children to suicide. But this article has also brought me in contact with another group of people, namely those who are contemplating suicide.

I didn't anticipate this, so when I first began hearing from such folk I was a little overwhelmed. *What should I say? I've never been down that road.* The temptation was to say nothing and hope that other readers might weigh in on the discussion threads. But I realized that was a cop-out and if I didn't speak up who knew what might happen. These were desperate people. They needed help now.

At the risk of sounding dramatic, I saw this as my Esther-moment. "Who knows, but maybe I've come to this position for such a time as this" (Esther 4:14). (Clearly I had forgotten the other part of that verse: "If you remain silent at this time, relief and deliverance will arise from another place.")

I began to encourage these folk by telling them how God has met me during the dark times of my own life. I spoke to dissuade them of the lie that says "this is all there is and nothing's going to change," and I sought to reveal the living hope that they have in Jesus Christ.

That E2R would become a sort of suicide helpline was unexpected, but I'm glad it happened. Grace is for the needy and who is more needy than the person ready to take their own life? And grace is also the perfect antidote for those who are beating themselves half to death in the name of religion.

I heard from one lady who had grown up in the church. She was so worn out from doing good that she had become depressed to the point of attempting suicide. That she should fall so low came as a great shock. "Suicide's a sin," she told me. "I never thought I would attempt that." Good, hard-working Christians never expect to become suicidal.

Yet Paul said the law condemns and ministers death (2 Corinthians 3:7–9). Try and live under the law and death is a very real possibility (see Romans 7:9).

Happily, this particular lady heard the gospel of grace and was delivered from performance-based Christianity. She is now convinced that the grace message is saving lives, especially Christian lives. I totally agree.

15. Star Trek and the Great Commission: Twelve Parallels

Today, September 8, is the anniversary of the first regular episode of *Star Trek*. How could I pass up an opportunity like this to talk about a cultural classic and one of my all-time favorite TV shows?

"But Paul, aren't you supposed to be writing about Bible stuff? What does one of the most culturally influential TV shows have to do with the grace of God?"

Um, not very much if I'm honest.

But if you stay up late with a bottle of Romulan ale and let your mind wander onto the bridge of the USS Enterprise, you might discover some amazing parallels between Starfleet's ongoing mission of exploration and our ongoing mission of preaching the good news. You might find that we have quite a few things in common with Captain Kirk, Mr. Spock, Bones, Scotty, et al.

For instance, have you ever noticed that the basic premise of *Star Trek* comes straight out of the New Testament? Think about it. Each week a starship captain descends from the heavens bringing good news and blessings to an isolated planet. Doesn't that remind you of another man who descended from heaven bringing good news to this orphaned planet?

I know, it's a stretch, but bear with me. This could be fun.

For all you Trekkies and Trekkers out there, here are twelve things Christians have in common with *Star Trek*:

1. We're on a mission. Like the crew of the Enterprise, we've got a job to do (Matthew 28:19). We might differ in what we define as good news, but we're both called to *go and tell*. There's no fluffing around on a starship. A sense of being on an exciting mission removes any inclination towards apathy.

2. Our desire is for the lost and unreached. Like Paul (Romans 15:20) and Captain Kirk, we're boldly going where no one has gone before.

3. We're on a quest for new life. Captain Kirk famously said he was seeking out new life. So are we (Acts 5:20). What does new life look like? *Christ in you*. In him is life (John 1:4) and whoever has the Son has life (1 John 5:12). We're like mothers in childbirth longing to see Christ formed in you (Galatians 4:19).

4. We're ambassadors. Like the crew of the Enterprise, we don't come in our own name but as representatives of another (2 Corinthians 5:20). We have no agendas or ministries of our own for we have been entrusted with the Lord's ministry of reconciliation (2 Corinthians 5:18). Our aim is to represent Jesus well.

5. We come in peace. Just as you won't see the Starship Enterprise firing wantonly on a new planet, you won't find us marching into town like scary Old Testament prophets (see 1 Samuel 16:4). Our feet are shod with the gospel of peace as we herald peace on earth and God's favor to men (Ephesians 6:15).

6. We're servant-hearted. The clever engineers and scientists on a starship can fix the village well and do whatever else needs to be done. Likewise, we minister to the whole person. The first words you might hear us say are, "What do you need?" We who were once servants of sin are now your servants for his sake (2 Corinthians 4:5).

7. We heal the sick. In the world of the Federation, Starfleet medical officers possess amazing healing powers, but I've never seen any of them resurrect the dead or drive out demons. We have superior capabilities and healing the sick is a part of our mission (Mark 16:18).

8. We're color-blind. On a starship bridge it doesn't matter if you're black or white, yellow or Vulcan. Everyone's in this together. Similarly, there is neither Jew nor Greek for we are all one in Christ (Galatians 3:28). Forty years ago *Star Trek* shocked the world with an interracial kiss. Big deal. Two

thousand years ago righteousness and peace kissed at the cross and everything changed (Psalm 85:10). The Righteous One embraced unrighteous humanity in the greatest act of love the world has ever seen (Romans 5:8).

9. We function best as a team. Contrary to his image as a maverick captain, James T. Kirk wouldn't last five minutes by himself. If the Enterprise is to leave space dock he's going to need Scotty, Spock, Bones and many others. It's the same with us (Romans 12:5). We're members of a body and each part is necessary (1 Corinthians 12:22). A lone Christian is about as useful as a starship captain on an empty bridge.

10. We work for free. Here's something you'll never see at the end of a *Star Trek* episode: a Starfleet officer handing a bill for services to a local official. It's the same with us (2 Thessalonians 3:8). Yes, we have to eat, but he who provides seed to the sower and bread for food takes care of us (2 Corinthians 9:10).

11. We shine in impossible situations. Like Captain Kirk we are not intimidated by overwhelming odds. We laugh in the face of adversity (Matthew 17:20). Unlike Kirk we don't survive by our wits and resourcefulness but by trusting in a mighty God who raises the dead (2 Corinthians 1:9).

12. We're not afraid of Klingons. In fact, we who have already died are not afraid of anything. The most repeated instruction in our operating manual is "fear not" (e.g., Isaiah 43:1).

A word after

There's an urban legend that says the Bible has been translated into the fictional *Star Trek* language of Klingon. This isn't true; only bits of it have been translated. But it does make you wonder what the gospel would sound like if preached in Klingon. The Klingons are a warrior race after all. I'm not sure they have words for peace, love, and forgiveness. I find it easier to picture Klingons reciting the Ten Commandments and the sundry laws of Moses. The imperative "thou shalt not" has an aggressive, Klingony feel about it, don't you think?

If there are any Klingon translators reading this I encourage you to concentrate your efforts on Leviticus. Trust me, it's a winning strategy. But to articulate the gospel of grace we need a better language, one that has multiple words for love. Greek, for instance. That could work.

Incidentally, Biblical Greek is recognized as a classical language which seems appropriate since it was used to convey a classic message. We have spent this whole book unpacking that message, but the message itself is not complicated. The gospel is simple. To demonstrate, let me finish with Paul's summary of it, as it appears in his classic greeting:

χάρις ὑμῖν καὶ εἰρήνη ἀπὸ Θεοῦ Πατρὸς ἡμῶν καὶ Κυρίου Ἰησοῦ Χριστοῦ ἀμήν.

Grace and peace to you from God our Father and the Lord Jesus Christ. Amen!

If you enjoyed this book, why not subscribe to E2R and get more articles just like these sent to your email. It's free! Sign up at:

escapetoreality.org/subscribe

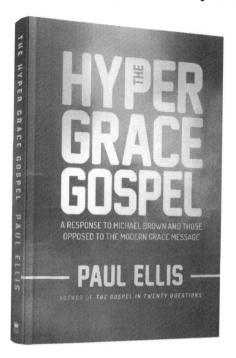

12390284R00063

Printed in Great Britain
by Amazon.co.uk, Ltd.,
Marston Gate.